Looking for a God To Pray To

Christian Spirituality in Transition

William Reiser, S.J.

PAULIST PRESS
New York and Mahwah, N.J.

IMPRIMI POTEST:
Very Rev. William A. Barry, S.J.
Provincial
Society of Jesus of New England

Scriptural quotations are taken from the
New Revised Standard Version Bible

Library of Congress Cataloging-in-Publication Data

Reiser, William E.
    Looking for a God to pray to : Christian spirituality in
transition / William Reiser.
        p.   cm.
    Includes bibliographical references.
    ISBN 0-8091-3480-2 (pbk.)
    1. Prayer—Christianity. 2. Spirituality—Christianity
I. Title
BV210.2.R38   1994
248—dc20   94-10552
                                                CIP

Published by Paulist Press
997 Macarthur Boulevard
Mahwah, NJ 07430

Printed and bound in the
United States of America

Contents

PART THREE: GETTING OUR BEARINGS
IN A TIME OF TRANSITION

Dedication:

For my students, past and present: *Ut cognoscant te, solum Deum verum et quem misisti Iesum Christum* (John 17:3). Which is inscribed above the Dinand Library at the College of the Holy Cross.

And for Albe and Julio, my godsons.

I imagine that a few hundred years hence there will be found to exist in the intellectual ideas which we shall have left behind us much that is contradictory; people will wonder how we put up with it. They will find much hard and dry husk in what we took for the kernel; they will be unable to understand how we could be so short-sighted, and fail to get a sound grasp of what was essential and separate it from the rest. Some day the knife will be applied and pieces will be cut away where as yet we do not feel the slightest inclination to distinguish. Let us hope then that we may find fair judges, who will measure our ideas not by what we have unwittingly taken over from tradition and are neither able nor called upon to correct, but by what was born out of our very own, by the changes and improvements which we have effected in what was handed down to us or was commonly prevalent in our day.

—Adolf Harnack
From *What is Christianity?*

Preface

The word "spirituality" has become problematic for some people today. To them, it suggests a dichotomy between the world of the spirit and the material or everyday world. "Spirituality" seems to consign matters such as prayer and contemplation, worship, growth in the virtues, and so forth, to the private, interior realm. Almost by definition, the realm of the spirit is considered to be higher than the world of the body. Spirituality, the objection runs, connotes distance from the tangible, everyday world and its pressing concerns, as if this world were religiously or humanly inferior to the nobler, more exalted realm of the interior life, namely, the life of the soul, which is preeminently the business of monks and contemplatives.

I have never felt uncomfortable with the term "spirituality," although I appreciate the limitations of the word. For me, "spirituality" refers to that which is properly human about us. We would not be fully created, fully human, apart from the image and likeness of God which has been impressed upon us from the beginning. We are only human to the extent that we are of and in the Spirit, since the Spirit is the source of our life. We are not fully made all at once; we become fully human over a lifetime. Consequently, spirituality refers to our ongoing creation, our continuing growth and development in the Spirit. This development takes us through the well-known categories of sin and grace, of purgation and freedom, of conversion and salvation, each of which names a familiar dimension of our experience. The things of the Spirit are nothing less than our opportunities for coming to fuller life and of becoming ever more completely and happily human.

The subtitle of this book, "Christian Spirituality in Transition," refers to three things. We are concerned with the specifically Christian

1

orientation of our humanity. We are not in the process of becoming Buddhists or Hindus or Muslims or Jews; each of these represents a distinctive way of being religious and, I would venture to say, even a distinctive way of being human. Following Jesus, however, is going to shape our humanity in a way which is both distinctive and particular. The choice, therefore, to become or to remain a Christian is really a choice about the kind of human being we want to be.

"Spirituality" refers to the unfolding, day by day, of that fundamental decision to become or to remain a Christian which we make at baptism, repeat at confirmation, and renew each time we receive the eucharist. What actually happens to those whose lives are essentially a matter of "being-with-Jesus"? What, concretely, takes place as they allow the Spirit to reign in their hearts and minds? What crises do they face? How do they deepen or develop their being-with-Jesus? How do they set about interpreting their lives and their experience? What sort of mission and ideals do they set for themselves? What is the mystery of God like for someone who has consciously chosen to follow Christ and to live the gospel? These are the questions which indicate what spirituality is all about.

By adding "in Transition" I want to draw attention to the fact that our becoming fully human does not occur in a timeless vacuum; it takes place within the concrete circumstances of our location in history. And our time and place within history, like those of the generations which have gone before us, are distinctive. We are not people of the Enlightenment or the Renaissance. We are not living in the Middle Ages, or in New Testament times. We do not belong to the generation which had to digest the news that the earth could be circumnavigated, or that our planet does not lie at the center of the universe. Actually, we are a people between worlds: the world of the late twentieth century and the dawning of a new era. Whether one wants to approach the future with optimism and confidence is ultimately a personal choice, but the fact is that something new is definitely in the process of being born.

The Second Vatican Council marked a decisive turning point in the history of the modern church, the importance of which may prove to surpass that of any previous council, although we cannot overlook the fact that Vatican II did not happen apart from what was going on in the rest of the world. Without the conditions of the modern world, Vatican II would have had neither direction nor shape. By 1962, the year in which the council opened, the world itself appeared to have reached another crucial turn as human consciousness finally appropriated the fact of modernity with its complex burdens of responsibility and guilt. Vatican II, in fact, represented a dramatic and long-overdue recognition of the world, its diverse cultures, its democratic aspirations, its technological genius, its scientific outlook, its essentially historical character, its non-Christian yet venerable religious traditions, and even its proclivity to atheism. In the years since the council, something else has been added to this list, namely, a thoroughgoing awareness of human poverty and the various forms of tyranny and injustice which both create poverty and keep it alive.

To say that Christian spirituality is in transition is merely to state the obvious fact that our sense of ourselves and of the mystery of God is undergoing profound change. The way that we think about and express our belief is being affected daily, even as we engage one another in these pages, by social and cultural pressures and events, by discoveries about how human beings interpret the world and God's action within it, and by the throbbing sounds of the world's poor crying for justice and a fair share of the goods of this earth. Even as the geopolitical maps have had to be redrawn in the wake of the breakup of the Soviet empire, so that the world now looks different than it did to most of us when we were in grammar school, so also our religious and theological maps are being redrawn in the light of countless developments: our increased understanding of scripture, our growing understanding of and respect for the other great religious traditions of the world, our attentiveness to the clamor of minorities to be heard and treated as people of God, fairly and with love. These are the new points which need to be incorporated into our spiritual maps.

We can no longer draw a map which clearly (and defensively) establishes borders between Catholics and Protestants; even the boundaries between Christianity and the other world religions are becoming less defined. We cannot draw a map which excludes women from participating fully in the ministerial life of the church. We cannot draw a map that would allow the lines between the rich and the poor to remain fixed. We cannot draw a map which visually positions Rome at the center of things, in the way that most world maps hanging on our classroom walls situated North America in the center.

Transition, then, means that what once was can no longer be. In fact, it will no longer be. And, to speak in gospel terms, any effort to redirect the crosscurrents of our time so that we could maintain things as they used to be would be reminiscent of those early Christians who refused to leave Jerusalem because they expected Jesus to return imminently and set all things straight. Jerusalem was destroyed, and the Temple upon which they pinned their hopes of a great restoration was torn down. The Spirit of Jesus was about to lead his followers and companions through the world, through all times and places. Ever after, the only fixed temple would be the human heart itself, as Jesus said (Jn 4:23–24). Nothing made by human hands, or crafted by human design, could satisfy that elusive quest for security that leads some people, now and then, to want to pitch camp and sink lasting roots into the earth.

Even the desire to erect a permanent dwelling place for God is misplaced. God neither needs nor requires a house. This might make us nervous, since we cannot conceive living securely without one. Maybe God's yielding to David's request that Israel be allowed to build a temple was a mistake on God's part (1 Chr 17). I mean no irreverence here; we are dealing, after all, with human stories about God. Yet David, Solomon and the whole people of Israel might have done better to meditate seriously on their ancient confession, which began, "A wandering Aramean was my ancestor . . ." (Deut 26:5). Certainly, for people who know the God of Israel (who is the God of Jesus), the experience of transition and impermanence should not be surprising. The God of Israel lived in a tent (1 Chr 17:5); the Son of Man had no place to lay his head (Lk 9:58). In short, immovability does not appear to be a divine attribute.

In the pages that follow, I have tried to make sense of what has been happening, at least from within the narrow confines of one person's perspective. The one feature which stands out as I look back over the last thirty years or so is transition: nothing turned out quite as I expected. Being a believer has been like playing a game in which the rules were changed almost without warning. Either the world changed, or the church changed, or people around me changed, none of which I

had any control over. And as a result, I changed, too: not merely in a
passive away, as if continually reacting to what has been going on
around me, but also as a thinking person who continues to hold that
faith and reason, nature and grace, the human spirit and the divine
Spirit, belong together inseparably.

The Plan of the Book

The book consists of an introduction, three parts, and a conclusion. The introduction is intended to prepare the reader for the reflections which follow by tracing some of the threads of transition. Although there I lean heavily upon my own experience, I believe that the
sense of being a transitional Christian is something many of us share.
Each of us could add another detail to the account, but on the whole
we would probably agree that one religious era seems to have ended
and a new one is emerging, although it is impossible to predict its
definitive form and shape.

The central thesis of the book is that tomorrow's prayer is going to
be different. It will involve a new way of conceiving the activity of
praying, a new way of imagining ourselves in relation to God, and a
new way of thinking about how God approaches us. Behind the individual reflections which comprise each of the three parts there lies a
question. These are meant to draw the reader's attention to consider
the following proposal, which may be more forcefully formulated in
interrogative terms: Can a Christian relate to the God of Jesus apart
from a conversion which leads one to think, choose and act preferen-
tially on behalf of the poor? Is Christian prayer essentially a matter of
living in relationship to the God of Jesus as a result of being with and
for the poor in our affections, loyalties and choices? Does Christian
prayer prove itself in the way that we surmount being pressured by
society to consume and to purchase? In the way that we seek to promote social and political change which serves the interests of oppressed
and impoverished people both at home and abroad? In the way that we
actively resist every effort to lord it over another through the abuse of
power (Mt 20:25)? Is the activity of prayer fundamentally a matter of
words spoken to God, or are the words simply manifestations or reflec-

tions of a basic posture, consciously chosen, of being in God's presence together with the entire human family, but particularly with the human family which continues to endure crucifixion? And do we arrive at this level through shutting the doors of our rooms and conversing with God in isolation? Or do we reach it through listening to the story of Jesus, and meditating upon it, through the optic of poor and oppressed people?

Perhaps I have raised too much to be gulped at once. But these are the main questions, and they help to establish the Christian coordinates of tomorrow's prayer. In the conclusion I have attempted to draw the book's main ideas together and address several concerns which could still be lingering in the reader's mind.

About ten years ago I read, and wrote a review of, Mark Taylor's *Erring: A Postmodern A/theology*, the first postmodern theology book I had ever come across.[1] The book left me absolutely bewildered. "Bleak" was the only word I could use to describe what seemed to lie ahead, if postmodernism should prove to be presaging things to come. "Gone are the images and stories which center Christian imagination," I wrote in the review. "Gone too are the notions of personal presence, providence, and salvation history which stabilize Christian practice." The book brought to mind some lines from the play, *A Man for All Seasons*, in which Thomas More was explaining to his impetuous son-in-law why he would give the Devil himself the benefit of the law:

> This country's planted thick with laws from coast to coast—man's laws, not God's—and if you cut them down—and you're just the man to do it—d'you really think you could stand upright in the winds that would blow then? Yes, I'd give the Devil benefit of law, for my own safety's sake.[2]

A world without story would be like a landscape in which all the trees had been axed. How then would we stand against the gale that would blow us to the edge of the earth? Annie Dillard had sized up things much better, reflecting upon probabilities and chance:

> And we need reminding of what time can do, must only do; churn out enormity at random and beat it, with God's blessing, into our

heads: that we are created, *created*, sojourners in a land we did not make, a land with no meaning of itself and no meaning we can make for it alone. Who are we to demand explanations of God? (And what monsters of perfection should we be if we did not?) We forget ourselves, picnicking: we forget where we are. There is no such thing as a freak accident. "God is at home," says Meister Eckhart, "We are in the far country."[3]

Some facts just stare us straight in the eye. Indeed, we live in a land "with no meaning of itself," as a postmodern individual might say. Nevertheless, the obvious thing about us is often the most overlooked, for this is also a "land we did not make." It is not by accident that we indulge in stories; we are already characters in the middle of a great one, which is daily unfolding before our very eyes. I have no idea whether postmodern thinking will find a lasting place among us; it may prove to be nothing but a symptom of the failure of nerve among first-world people. But I do think that if in the future there are still going to be Christians among us who know how to pray, then, like workers reseeding a wounded forest, we shall have to make sure that we do not forget how to hand on our stories of God.

An Acknowledgment

I would like to thank Paul Harman, S.J., for reading an earlier draft of this book and encouraging me even then to have it published. I am also grateful to James F. X. Pratt, S.J., for suggesting needed clarifications; he proved to be a loyal yet helpfully critical reader. I should also thank Michael Gareffa, S.J., for steering me in the direction of authors and titles I would not ordinarily come across. Kenneth Scott and Robert Henry, Jr., the Microcomputer Support Specialists at Holy Cross, once again showed their patience and wizardry as I continue making the transition from typewriter to microchips. I am especially grateful to many former students who sat through lectures where I attempted to articulate for the first time the ideas discussed here, and who prodded my thinking further by voicing many of their religious questions, doubts, aspirations and experiences.

Introduction

Reviewing the Spiritual Landscape

One evening last summer I was astonished to discover that our local Barnes & Noble bookstore had allocated twenty-four shelves to the category "New Age" spirituality. Many of the titles baffled me; they read like hybrids of astrology and science fiction. In fact, the section immediately following included books on astrology and the occult, which is where some bookstores prefer to stock religious titles! A few of the New Age rituals, which were designed to foster personal wholeness and communion with the earth spirits, sounded spooky. I learned, though, that the best of this writing offers routes to inner peace and healing, oneness with the cosmos and self-acceptance, and even talks about God. As I was mumbling under my breath about the number of works in front of me, a young woman grabbed a book from the shelf and found the page she wanted. "Look," she was explaining to her friend, "this is what we're here for, to find ourselves."[1]

I was too timid to ask her to show me the passage, yet I could not help but think of the gospel text which says, in effect, that the person who wants to save his life is going to lose it; the one who loses her life for Jesus' sake, which is to say, for the sake of others, is going to find it (Mk 8:35). The salesclerk later told me that New Age material had attracted quite a readership. But why, I was wondering, were people turning to things like New Age spirituality? Has the gospel nothing to offer them? What has happened, that the mystery of God should be reduced to a matter of feeling good about oneself and benevolent toward all creatures? The sad thing to me was not that the Christian tradition was lacking in satisfying forms of prayer and meditation, since there is a wealth of material in the tradition to aid those seeking to deepen their interior life, grow in self-knowledge and center their hearts on the mystery of God. What saddened me was that many people do not seem to have developed a spirituality which is informed by the story of Jesus.

I think, too, of a friend from the seminary whose search for wholeness and tranquility of soul led him to the Dalai Lama, and eventually to embrace Buddhism. And I have observed some young Catholics become so entranced with Zen centering exercises that they ultimately wound up forsaking their ancestral faith. This happened partly because the church's rituals, doctrines and piety had left them unmoved, or even at times disaffected, and partly because they had discovered that there are other avenues to inner directedness and peace besides what Christianity claims to provide.

While there is obviously much that is good and helpful that does not go by the name of Christian, where, I ask myself, has Christianity failed these people? Have they really known the gospel story? Has it challenged them to the depths of their souls? Please do not misunderstand me. I am not threatened by the fact that some people leave the church, although I am often pained by it. After all, there were many who heard Jesus who chose not to follow him. Perhaps in some cases it is even more salutary that some people do "leave" the church, if in the process they eventually find God. Perhaps it was better for the prodigal son that he did walk out of his father's house, since only after he was away in a "distant country" did he begin to experience real want and come to a profound realization of what he had once possessed. Sometimes I explain at the beginning of a theology lecture that no one *has* to be a Christian. Following Jesus is always invitational. Being Christian does not abrogate a person's God-given freedom to choose the basic orientation of his or her life. Nevertheless, I also believe that it is important for people to know who this Jesus is whom they choose to follow, or not to follow. And how will they know, unless they "come and see"? (Jn 1:39)

The same point struck me from an altogether different direction when a young Hispanic in his late twenties asked me to send him, in prison, a copy of the Koran. I knew him and his family very well, having been with them through baptisms, wakes and funerals. Behind the prison walls he apparently had discovered a militantly fervent Islamic brotherhood to replace the softness of the Christianity he had known all his life. There was a firmness and purposefulness in his voice I had never heard in him before.

Once again I began wondering how Christian faith had failed him and the other members of his new brotherhood, most of whom would have come, at least culturally, from Christian backgrounds. Was there nothing militant about the gospel? Was there nothing in the story of Jesus to attract young people, alienated from the larger society, which could provide them with challenge, purpose and mission? Why trade the cross—that most revolutionary of signs, that great protest against injustice—for an armband, or a tattoo, or a haircut? Why should the Koran come to symbolize the struggle against social oppression, instead of the cross? Does the story of Jesus have nothing to say to the immense frustration of those trapped at the bottom of society? Does the cross reveal everything about forgiveness and nothing about justice? Is it a sign of submission, or is it the sign of a prophet's protest? In short, is there nothing revolutionary about Christian spirituality?

One thing seemed clear to me, however. There is more protest, more defiance against the tyranny of evil and injustice, in the Psalms, and indeed in the gospel story, than in New Age spirituality.

At any rate, the thirst for a deeper interior life is evident in other popular writings besides the New Age material, nearly all of which can be found among the other shelves of a decent bookstore. One can usually find, of course, the works of past masters, such as Thomas à Kempis' *The Imitation of Christ*, Francis de Sales' *Introduction to the Devout Life*, and the anonymously written *The Cloud of Unknowing*; occasionally, too, *The Dark Night of the Soul* from the sixteenth-century mystic John of the Cross, and maybe a collection of the writings of Meister Eckhart. But you can also spot works from contemporary masters like *The Seven Storey Mountain* of Thomas Merton (1948) and Dorothy Day's *The Long Loneliness* (1952). In addition, there are a number of recent works which really could qualify as spiritual reading: Nancy Mairs' refreshingly feminist autobiographical reflection *Ordinary Time*,[2] some of the meditative pieces of Annie Dillard,[3] and Patricia Hampl's *Virgin Time: In Search of the Contemplative Life*.[4] Each of these authors demonstrates the ability sometimes to evoke experience, sometimes to clarify it, so that the reader can affirm without shame or timidity the worth and sacredness of his or her own life.[5]

The current interest in prayer and fostering a personal relationship with God is similarly reflected in respected writers such as Emilie Griffin,[6] Basil Pennington,[7] Henri Nouwen[8] and William Barry.[9] The success of a book like Thomas Moore's *Care of the Soul: A Guide for Cultivating Depth and Sacredness in Everyday Life* testifies further to the widespread hunger in our society for a deeper spiritual life and a greater understanding of how one develops "soulfulness."[10] And, by way of contrast, Kenneth Leech's *Eye of the Storm: Living Spirituality in the Real World* sounds an important caution against retreating into a cultivation of the interior life apart from an engagement with the world.[11]

One particularly appealing feature of contemporary spiritual writing is the enormous attention being given to the experiences of men and women who are seriously attempting to lead good Christian lives in a world and in a culture which has thrown at them many challenges and stumbling blocks. For all its optimism, and for all its appreciation of the accomplishments of modern culture through science and technology, the council was hardly naive about the harsh reality of sin. Sin ultimately is the sole reason for the vast inequalities which exist throughout the world, the aggression and torture inflicted by one group upon another, and the poverty and hunger which have butchered countless men, women and children. Yet where sin abounds, so does grace (Rom 5:20). And in that perennial dialectic between sin and grace, which affects both individual human beings as well as their societies and institutions, men and women continue to encounter the holy mystery of God. That encounter, so embedded in the business and routine of the everyday world, generates what is properly called religious experience.

As writers and thinkers have investigated and reflected upon that experience, the term "experience" has itself achieved nearly canonical status. *Experience* confirms the truths of our faith; *experience* provides the interpretative key which unlocks all sorts of meaning within the ancient biblical texts. Theological investigation which bears no relationship to the *experience* of the believing community is likely to be labeled irrelevant, while theologians who speak or write about God, but who themselves have little or no *experience* of the matters about which they write, might be considered to have been less than faithful to their calling. In other words, apart from experience theology is dead. And in particular theology and contemporary spirituality have become increasingly sensitive to the experience of the poor and those whose voices have generally not been heard.[12]

The fact that human experience is both a rich and indispensable source for sound spirituality has probably nowhere been demonstrated more clearly than in Latin America. Works such as Gustavo Gutierrez' *We Drink from Our Own Wells*[13] and Ernesto Cardenal's *The Gospel in Solentiname* in which he assembled the shared scriptural reflections of village people in Nicaragua[14] are notable examples. The fact that experience must be carefully noticed precisely because God moves and speaks there, in the ordinary rhythms of our lives, may very well be the explanation for the resurgence of interest in spiritual direction over the last two decades.[15] Retreat houses, together with courses and institutes for training spiritual directors, have multiplied and continue to attract many religiously earnest individuals. All this movement continues to flow naturally from the church-wide renewal initiated by Vatican II.

It would be a well-nigh impossible task to assemble all the voices, themes and insights of the spiritual writers who dominated the Catholic scene in the decades prior to the council, and it would be equally difficult, even foolhardy, to attempt to survey all the developments within Christian spirituality which have occurred since then. The one thing we can be sure of is that Catholics still possess an abiding interest in cultivating the interior life, or the life of grace, as we used to say. If I had to select the two major changes that have occurred within our piety over the last thirty years, I would submit that they are, first, a way of conceiving our relationship to God which is more communal and less private; and secondly, a way of relating to Jesus which dwells more on his humanness than his divinity.

I would also submit that anyone researching the period stretching, say, from 1950 through 1990 would notice that Christian spirituality had been in transition during that entire period, largely as a result of numerous social and cultural forces and historical events over which the church had no control. At Vatican II the church acknowledged, in effect, that its attitude toward the world and modern culture had been far too defensive, and that it could never hope to effect change in a world it could neither speak with nor understand. Although many other influences were certainly at work in conciliar theology, Pierre Teilhard de Chardin's *Divine Milieu: An Essay on the Interior Life* (appearing in English in 1960), which was at the time a bold departure from the traditional treatises on Christian asceticism, helped to chart the course for a new spiritual future (in fact, some people regard Teilhard as one of the pioneers of New Age spirituality). Christian spirituality would become creation-centered, and believers would henceforth regard the world far more positively and reverently than they had ever consciously done before. The goodness of creation is perhaps the major theme running through the work of Matthew Fox, another well-known writer. For him, materiality is not something to be suspicious about or eschewed; it should be celebrated.[16] After all, the creed did not profess a spiritual resurrection, but a bodily one; and the Word had not become angelic spirit; it had become flesh.

The human thirst for wholeness, founded in a person's and in a community's relationship to God, has been the indelible character on the soul of our common humanity. That character was imprinted, as it were, through the sacrament of creation and cannot be erased by human hands. Spirituality, therefore, should be as natural to us as breathing. It is as hard to imagine adulthood without spirituality as it would be to think of growing up without ever falling in love.

Faith-in-Transition: A Personal Note

The realization that we are transitional Christians, that is, followers of Jesus who are living in the midst of enormously powerful and largely unpredictable historical crosscurrents, has occupied my thinking for over twenty years. The idea first struck me forcefully in the late 1960's and early 1970's. These were the years just before my ordination and just after Vatican II. Between the time I entered the seminary and the time I was ordained, so many things had happened in the world at large and within the church that I honestly had no idea how deeply my understanding of ministry, sacraments, prayer, church, morality and even my view of the action of God in the world had been affected.

To this day, men and women in my parent's generation can recall where they were and what they were doing on December 7, 1942, the day of the attack on Pearl Harbor. Although the exact moment can hardly be pinpointed the same way, I believe that many of us can similarly recall where we were and what we were like in 1962, what being Catholic meant to us then, on the eve of the Second Vatican Council. And just as that fateful attack galvanized the political will of the nation, so too the wind which suddenly swept over the church would leave us resolved to settle for nothing less than a thoroughgoing renewal of the religious institution to which we had dedicated our lives. It is important for those of us who were alive at the time to recall what sort of Christians we were, in order to appreciate the great transition through which we are currently living. And it may be just as important for those who were born after the council to listen to our stories and anecdotes. After all, grasping what it means to be Christian is not like getting the digital readout on a watch. Time includes a past and a future; so does our faith.

The two key events in my lifetime which shook loose the trusting way I approached the twin worlds of church and society were the publication of Paul VI's encyclical *Humanae Vitae* (or rather, the letter's reception by the Catholic world) and the Vietnam War. The first forced me to consider whether the Holy Spirit was actually guiding the institutional church. How could things have reached such a pass that the pope could be on one side of an issue and so many good people on the other? The second awakened me to the realization that none of us could afford to take our citizenship passively. These events spelled the end of religious and political innocence; an old era was breaking up. But many other things happened, too. [17]

If I had to state the one single development which occurred during the past forty years that has mattered to me more than anything else, I would say that it is that we appreciate better that the gospel belongs to all of us. Not just to priests, or to the sisters, or to the monks, or to the missionaries, but to all of us. The impact of this development may be hard to gauge, but this is the point at which everything comes together. The liturgical changes prompted by Vatican II, not to mention the council's inspired openness to the world's cultures and to history, the great doctrinal renewal which the council set in motion, and the breathtaking developments in Catholic biblical studies over the past fifty years, all converge on one point: that the gospel is the spiritual heritage of all Christians, and every aspect of our faith has to be centered accordingly.

As we learn more about the gospel, and about the story of Jesus, we can understand why the piety and devotional practices of our youth are hopelessly outdated. At root there was a very different version of the story of Jesus. The older version had been shaped and handed on by churchmen, by the institutional apprentices who sincerely believed that they were communicating the real story of Jesus. I do not mean that these instructors included sayings or events in the story which were not actually there, or that they omitted things which were there. Rather, I believe, they failed to impress upon us what the story of Jesus really *meant*. Sometimes they sounded as if Jesus' sole concern was founding a church, and this implied that the church was supposed to be the center of everybody's life, just as it was for the clergy.[18]

When I ask myself what the points of continuity are between the faith I practiced through adolescence and as a young adult, and what I practice today, I find that very little has remained intact. The blessed sacrament, which played such a central role in my early piety, now features less prominently both in my thinking and in my activities, than the Christian community itself: it is more important that we form and renew our community life than that we concentrate on the planning and celebration of eucharistic liturgies, although I sincerely believe that sacramental celebrations have a necessary place in the life of a community that wants to grow in the spirit of Jesus. I want to find God, but the tabernacle is not a likely place to expect to meet the God who takes flesh "in the features of men's faces." The notion of doctrine feels less important to me than the gospel story of Jesus. I am less drawn to want to present and explain the church's dogmas than I am drawn to helping people hear the story behind our faith. I am far more familiar with the weaknesses and failures of the institutional church than I was growing up, and far less impressed with the ecclesiastical bureaucracy.

While at an earlier time I would have been most concerned about understanding the person and identity of Jesus, today I find myself more concerned about understanding his mission, and his connection with the reign of God. It is his fidelity to the reign of God that confers on Jesus his proper role and identity in the ongoing story of our faith, rather than his one-to-one relationship with the Father. The title "son of God" is not what makes Jesus special; all of us are daughters and sons of God as well. His specialness arises from his association with the reign of God, and from his abiding trust that God would fulfill the divine promises made through the people of Israel to the whole human race. Jesus' specialness does not arise because he called God "Abba, Father"; his prayer was a consequence of his experience, not the cause of it. And, what was harder for me to admit, it is less important to me that I should be a priest than that I should be, in my imagination and in my prayer, a companion of Jesus. It is less important to me that all should embrace Christianity than that all should be able to live with the freedom and dignity of the children of God. It is less important to me to advance and defend the uniqueness of Christ and Christian belief, than it is to help people hear the story of God behind the story of Jesus.

The first thing the cross says to me is not that I have been redeemed; it does not tell me about God's love for this poor sinner. The cross has become, rather, a permanent sacramental reminder of the history of human oppression, the suffering endured by the poor and exploited peoples of the earth at the hands of the wealthy and powerful. It speaks to me of God's oneness with the suffering of people. The first thing the resurrection says to me is not that Jesus is the exalted Lord, but that God refuses to let the power of death have the last word or comment about the trustworthiness of the divine promise. Death does not put the final spin on Jesus' fidelity to the kingdom of God.

Today I have a clearer sense of the presence of God when I sit in the apartment of a poor family or on a bench in a busy park than when I sit in a quiet chapel before the tabernacle. I cannot dissociate God's presence from people; oneness with them in imagination and sympathy has supplanted my former sense of being alone with God. I can no longer be alone with God that way. My youthful approach to Christ's presence in the blessed sacrament on retrospect looks terribly naive, as naive as the effort of Mary Magdalene to hold on to the form of the earthly Jesus.

The prayer form to which I was finally drawn was a devout, unrushed reading of scripture. And here I made a wonderful discovery.

The scriptures are testaments of the faith experience of people over countless generations. In picking up the Bible, one has in one's hands the history of salvation and the great story of God's affair with the human race. Whenever I read the Bible, I do not sense that God is "speaking" to me, as if God had personally recorded the scriptural words, or as if God were trying to whisper words of life in my ear. Rather, each time I pick up the scriptures I feel as if the tradition has picked me up and invited me into humanity's great story about God: not just the God of the Christians, or the God of the Jews, but the God of all peoples in all times. When my eyes pass over the biblical texts, I am aware of the presence of untold believers and of a wordless belonging to the entire human family. It is like receiving communion.

The reason for taking time to sketch a little of the landscape of my religious past and present is not to indulge in autobiography for its own sake, and by no means is it meant to suggest that my experience should be normative of anyone else's. My purpose is simply to provide the reader with some idea of one person's social and spiritual "location," as it were, in the hope that the reader will identify with some of these moments and inner states as indications of a spirituality in transition. I come from a traditional Catholic family and I have appropriated over the years the traditional Catholic values and outlook upon the world which characterized those of us born shortly before the end of the Second World War, and whose basic spiritual outlook was formed prior to the Second Vatican Council.

The likely fact is that most of us are Catholic by habit. We think about the world in Christian terms. The existence and the presence of God are non-negotiable first principles for us; to deny them would be to renounce every claim to rationality. We further believe that Jesus is the Son of God, although we may be at a loss to account for this in precise conceptual terms. Maybe the only way to describe Jesus' specialness is from within the story of Israel's dealings with God, or of God's dealings historically with the people of Israel. We also hold the church to be an ark of salvation, because it keeps the possibility of our being a single human family illumined within human history. Indeed, this is the creator's desire for us. The church points in the direction of that profound communion which every human heart desires above all

The Church is the vehicle for our being a single human family. / communion

else. The church keeps reminding us of the promises which God has made to the world.

Several years ago, in the course of a seminar I was teaching on contemporary spirituality, I assigned my students *The Seven Storey Mountain*. Since this book had exercised a deep and lasting effect upon me and upon many others of my generation, I had hoped it would have a similar effect upon my students. It did not. And the reason was that Merton had successfully found meaningfulness in the very disordered life and time prior to and during the Second World War; he told the story about how one person had found peace and had made sense of the world.

The world Thomas Merton was trying to interpret, and which he finally grasped through the mystery and gift of faith, was very different from the world of students today. Their search for meaning is quite different from Merton's, or at least from the early Merton, the Merton of *The Seven Storey Mountain*. They were unable to relate to Merton's description of the church of his day, and they often failed to see how *that* church could have satisfied anybody's spiritual needs. It is with this in mind that I have included this personal note. Those reading these pages who were born after the council need to appreciate the issues which have shaped the outlook of those of us who want nothing more than to pass the gift of faith on to them.

Something new is about to be born, a way of being Christian which will be both continuous with the past and at the same time decidedly new. We are living within historical crosscurrents, a period of such immense forces that the changes we are undergoing are very difficult to measure, even at times to perceive. The overriding sense which many people have is the sense of collapse, of breakdown, of nihilism. The music teenagers from our inner cities have been listening to, for example, is profoundly chilling, and sounds a warning; the lyrics chronicle an experience of addiction, abuse, violence and death. For many of them, the future holds little else. For all of us, things are not the way they used to be, and thus some men and women finish out their days lamenting the loss of old securities. Even today, many people attend mass, not because the liturgy speaks to their deepest religious needs and experience, but because they want the reassurance that at least something never changes and is capable of withstanding the pressures and betrayals of our time. They desire and require a link with the past. They feel the need to stand outside of time, as it were, in order to have at least the semblance of touching again the mystery of the transcendent. No matter if the transcendent and holy mystery of God has slipped away from us; at least the outer form of that mystery—the liturgy as we have known it, and the sacrament reserved in our tabernacles—remains as a fixed point in stormy and uncharted seas. But will such an approach to our interior life work?

Perhaps this should be our starting point. Where do we encounter the mystery of God today? With so much talk about spirituality, prayer, and renewal, are we really that much closer to "discerning the mystery"? With all the changes which have taken place over the past thirty years, are we more firmly in touch with the mystery of God than we were before the council? Does the word "God" still speak to people today, or has God become both nameless and faceless, a philosophical abstraction, a "literary marker," or a relic from humanity's naive, superstitious past? Will the word "God" be out of place in a post-modern world?

The answer to these questions largely depends upon us. The notion of God is defined above all by the way men and women of God live. In the past, thinkers speculated about the meaning of God, as they searched the universe for an ultimate principle of order, truth, goodness and beauty. Their experience led them to probe the heavens. Today, the world has other proposals to account for the why and wherefore of things. In my view, the word "God" designates what the fourth gospel refers to as way, truth and life (Jn 14:6). The way is justice. The truth is compassion. The life is communion. As human beings incarnate justice, compassion and communion, they reveal what the mystery of God means *for us*. Through the way they live, they draw attention to the silent, empowering presence that has accompanied the world since its beginning.

In fact, perhaps the *notion* of God never did make much sense, as if "God" could be placed alongside all the other great ideas in the libraries of the world as a specimen of human speculative genius. In the biblical tradition, the word "God" has always been personal and relational: God-for-us. That is why it has been impossible to think of

God without thinking of the human race at the same time. To say "God" is immediately to wonder "God-for-whom?" To answer this, and again to appeal to our tradition, we probably ought to reply "God-for-the-poor." Find the poor, and you will find God. Find the poor, and one knows right away "Why justice?" Find the sin that causes human misery, and one knows right away "Why compassion?" Find the core desires of the human heart for love and acceptance, and one understands immediately "Why communion?" Except that in this case, communion remains incomplete until all can take their places at the same table, rich and poor alike. And it is the poor, finally, who offer the invitation to the great banquet, for to them has been promised the kingdom of God.

Living in a time of transition requires that we develop a spirituality which reflects our historical situation at the twilight of the twentieth century. Such a spirituality is going to entail a fresh way of conceiving and talking about our relationship to God, of praying, and of looking at the world. The pages which follow are simply one contribution in that direction. I hope that what I have written is clear, and I apologize in advance for whatever inadequacies or shortcomings the reader may discover there. After many years of meditation and dialoguing with believers from other world religions, Bede Griffiths, one of the spiritual pioneers of our time, expressed sentiments which might apply to a Christian spirituality in transition:

> Every human institution, every land or city or kingdom or temple or church is a "copy of a shadow," a manifestation in time and space of an eternal reality. The whole creation and all human history are "symbols" of a transcendent mystery. All religious doctrines are "myths" or symbolic expressions of a truth which cannot properly be expressed. Every form of priesthood and sacrifice, of ritual and sacrament, belongs to the world of "signs" which is destined to pass away. Today, more than ever, we are being called to recognize the limitations of every form of religion. Whether Christian or Hindu or Buddhist or Muslim, every religion is conditioned by time and place and circumstances. All their outward signs are destined to pass away. As a Muslim saying has it: "Everything passes save his face." But in all these outward forms of religion, of doctrine and sacrament and organization, the one eternal Truth is

revealing itself, the one Mystery is making itself known, the one transcendent Being is making itself manifest. Idolatry consists in stopping at the sign; true religion is the passing through the sign to the Reality. [19]

I am not sure that Griffiths would have agreed with me about where we must look to discover "the one eternal Truth," and I would reject any suggestion that the differences between the world religions could be leveled away (although I do not think that this is what he is really saying); but I share his sense that many things are passing. A person becoming familiar with God learns not to be afraid.

PART ONE
WHERE SHALL WE LOOK
FOR GOD?

1

The Passing of the
Torch of Faith

No one thinker influenced so deeply the shape of Catholic theology in the second half of our century as the German Jesuit Karl Rahner (1904–1984). Rahner opened up a way of thinking about Christian truth which liberated us from the dogmatism of the past and led us away from a form of theological reflection which had become a little too self-assured about its conclusions. The theological enterprise itself, Rahner had proven, was very much alive.

Rahner believed, of course, that our encounter with the holy mystery of God, and God's free, loving self-communication to us, can never be exhaustively described. The mystery and presence of God cannot be captured and confined by human language or concepts, and there is no way of infallibly determining where and when the divine reality will show itself in the future, for God is absolutely free. Nevertheless, we must try our best to put into words what is essentially beyond language, to name what is unnameable, since men and women will otherwise be unable to speak with one another about the one Reality which sets everything else into perspective. And since God may be present among us in the most unusual of places and circumstances, we must also keep discerning the "signs of the times" if we are ever to exclaim with relieved love, "It is the Lord!" (Jn 21:7) Through the symbols and stories of our faith, and even through the reflective language of theology itself, we discover the truth that points us toward God. In the end, however, theology is a humble science. Unlike other branches of human learning and inquiry, theology is healthiest when it acknowledges how little it knows. Yet if the time should come when human beings no longer attempt to speak about God, then humanity as we know it will have ended: "The absolute death of the word 'God,' including even the eradication of its past, would be the signal, no longer heard by anyone, that man himself had died."[1]

When Rahner died, it seemed as if a great light had gone out in the sky. For as long as Rahner was alive, somehow one felt safe from the assaults of those post-Vatican II forces which wanted to reverse the direction and possibilities opened up by the council, and one also felt that no matter what objection might be brought against Christian faith, from any corner, Rahner was there to answer it. How much this was the case came home to me one evening when, while browsing through a bookstore, I picked up Steven Weinberg's *Dreams of a Final Theory*. Weinberg, an eminent physicist, suggested that a person can quite plausibly live and die (and account for the existence of the universe) without the notion of God. He writes, "The more we refine our understanding of God to make the concept plausible, the more it seems pointless." With respect to the scientific community, he adds, "But as far as I can tell from my own observations, most physicists are not sufficiently interested in religion to qualify as practicing atheists." Apparently, the notion of God does little more than serve the emotional needs of the scientifically immature.[2]

I am old enough to listen to such claims without being threatened by them, and I know that there are other scientists who take a far more favorable view of religion,[3] but each time I come across views which challenge or even undermine the Christian story about God a sudden rush of uncertainty and doubt leaves me wishing that Rahner were still among us. One still awaits the Rahnerian word, explaining that the notion of God which is often rejected by scientifically enlightened people indeed *ought* to disappear. As Kenneth Leech warned, "To hold a false and inadequate view of God is more serious an obstacle to faith than atheism, and so the abandonment of false views is a necessary purifying element."[4] Theology, after all, does not begin as primitive science. The God of Israel, the God of Jesus, should not be identified with the First Cause or the Prime Mover of ancient philosophy and medieval theology. Faith's origins lie elsewhere.

In some ways, my dependency upon Rahner probably sounds immature. It is not unlike wishing that one's parents were still alive, for our parents (including our "theological parents") are our front-line defense against the hostile forces of life and the untamed powers of the future. Rahner wrote eloquently of God. Even when I did not understand what he was saying (this often happened), I was convinced that he really did know and experience the mystery of God. The fact that someone of Rahner's intelligence believed in God made those of us with lesser intellectual gifts more confident about our own belief. The rest of us could endure the uncertainties of a transitional age so long as religious giants were there, helping us to discern the mystery in our midst. In a thrilling essay in which Rahner addressed members of the Society of Jesus today by assuming the voice of the Society's founder, it was clear that while the person speaking was Ignatius Loyola, the sureness of the language was Rahner:

> But one thing is sure: after Manresa, from then on, I knew the inscrutable incomprehensibility of God ever more intensely, ever more purely. . . . God himself; I knew God himself, not simply human words describing him. I knew God and the freedom which is an integral part of him and which can only be known through him and not as the sum total of finite realities and calculations about them.[5]

The very words Rahner used often conveyed a sublimity of thought which struck me as unparalleled in Catholic theological literature. I found the same conviction about the reality and mystery of God in Rahner's writing as I had found in the opening pages of Augustine's *Confessions*:

> Who then are you, my God? What, I ask, but God who is Lord? For 'who is the Lord but the Lord,' or 'who is God but our God?' Most high, utterly good, utterly powerful, most omnipotent, most merciful and most just, deeply hidden yet most intimately present, perfection of both beauty and strength, stable and incomprehensible, immutable and yet changing all things, never new, never old, making everything new and 'leading' the proud 'to be old without their knowledge'; always active, always in repose, gathering to yourself but not in need, supporting and filling and protecting, creating and nurturing and bringing to maturity, searching

even though to you nothing is lacking: you love without burning,
you are jealous in a way that is free of anxiety, you 'repent' without
the pain of regret, you are wrathful and remain tranquil. You will a
change without any change in your design. You recover what you
find, yet have never lost.[6]

The voices of Rahner and Augustine have always sounded to me so
certain and so in touch with God. Yet the fact remains that our salvation is not going to be won through believing in God because they
believed in God, any more than children can be spared the experience
of growing up because their parents went through it ahead of them.
There comes a time when children must step into their parents' shoes
and become parents themselves. There comes a time when students
will take up where their teachers left off, and become teachers themselves. We call this growing up, and it applies to individuals and
communities alike.

Figures like Augustine and Rahner discovered, in their day, that
the mystery of God is at the same time the mystery of the human being:
behind the human story there lies a story of God. We cannot narrate
the one without telling the other. How in the world can we talk about
God, unless we know how to talk about ourselves? How can the mind
probe the heavens for traces of God if it has not first plumbed the
human mind itself? This is what Rahner did, and Augustine and
Aquinas before him. They studied and pondered the way human beings reason and feel and love. In the human mind and heart they
recognized the divine reflection itself, in whose image we had been
fashioned.

For us who are living through this time of transition, however,
perhaps the starting point for talking about God is less likely to be an
analysis of the human mind or the human heart, as it was for numerous Christian thinkers and contemplatives before us. Perhaps it is not
going to be our personal religious experience, either, as it was for
Ignatius Loyola and the great mystics of the Christian tradition. Once
again, figures like Ignatius and Teresa of Avila, Meister Eckhart and
Julian of Norwich, knew God, and they spoke out of a faith proven by
fire. But it simply will not do to persuade ourselves that because Christian faith has given rise to mystics, the existence of God is thereby

confirmed. Our faith is not solidly grounded, if its security is based in the mystical experience of holy giants. Vicarious experiences of God will not save us.

The lives of other Christians have provided models of faith in our time: Dorothy Day, Oscar Romero, Thomas Merton, Cesar Chavez, not to mention the everyday holiness we have frequently encountered among our families and friends. Taken together with countless "anonymous" believers throughout history, these men and women provide an impressive witness of humanity's thirst for the Spirit of Life. They have even helped to create the climate of faith which we still feel and respond to within the church. But there is no getting around the fact that at the close of the twentieth century we are in a very different place religiously and culturally from the men and women who walked ahead of us.

When they finally came to the end of their forty years of wandering, the people of Israel were unable to take Moses along with them, and this no doubt left them fearful and anxious. When the giants who have protected us pass away, the future can appear ominous. And Moses was indeed larger than life:

> Never since has there arisen a prophet in Israel like Moses, whom the Lord knew face to face. He was unequalled for all the signs and wonders that the Lord sent him to perform in the land of Egypt, against Pharaoh and all his servants and his entire land (Deut 34:10–11).

But Moses died, and the Spirit raised up Joshua. Yet the Pharaoh died, too, and the "land of Egypt" would eventually become only a memory. Before long there would be new opposition, and a different landscape: new dangers and new possibilities.

Like the people of Israel, every so often in the history of Christian faith men and women have faced frontiers. Some would resist crossing because they did not want to move. The past, no matter how dreadful, offered at least some measure of security: "Was it because there were no graves in Egypt that you have taken us away to die in the wilderness? What have you done to us, bringing us out of Egypt? . . . For you have brought us out into this wilderness to kill this whole assembly with hunger" (Ex 14:11; 16:3). Others were too old, or afraid, to undertake the passage. Still others would wander off in the wrong direction. Yet there were always some who put their faith in God, as Abraham had done many centuries ago, and Moses after him, and set out to find the place of promise.

"Place of promise" or "the promised land" is a metaphor, at least for the Christian imagination. For the people of Israel, the promised land meant a particular piece of real estate; they believed that God was about to give them the deed to that land in perpetuity. Christians have been less concerned with Israel's understanding of the divine promise and have instead tended to interpret the promised land, either spiritually, as the kingdom of heaven, or in this-worldly terms, as the reign of God. In both cases, the promised land carries a note of futurity. The realization of God's promise lies in the future, beyond our sight, but not beyond our power to trust. In the moment of passage, the human heart lives by hope. Armed only with the stories which remember the faith of those who have preceded them, every generation must travel the route of the exodus by itself. Each generation must discover the springs of faith anew, or it is doomed to die of thirst in the wilderness.

As the torch passes, we are forced to own the ancient faith for ourselves. The giants of the past have left us with signposts; they have bequeathed to us the witness of their own fidelity to the things of God, as they understood them. In the end, however, we have to strike out on our own and learn about God for ourselves. Our ancestors have left us the record of their experience, but their experience can never substitute for ours. We can read their books and ponder their example, yet until we encounter the empowering source of their writings and their actions, we shall be a people adrift, tossing about aimlessly in a sea of change.

2

Can the Ancient Truths
Still Guide Us?

The truths of our faith are often said to be timeless and immune from change. Like the divine mystery itself, the truths which have guided countless generations of believers are a rock in which they have taken refuge (Ps 18:2), a stronghold in time of trouble (Ps 9:9). Even though the earth should change and the mountains shake (Ps 46:2), the truths of faith remain a refuge for the mind and strength for the soul. Yet in a time of transition the reassurance that we possess the truth may offer meager protection against the currents of change. What might have appeared utterly obvious to one generation can be totally dismissed by another. What appears logical within one set of circumstances can look extremely muddled in another. Arguments for the existence of God, for example, held suasive force for an age raised to think that the universe is intelligibly ordered; but an age that does not honor reason because the world often shows itself to be so unreasonable, might find the existence of God anything but logical. A generation brought up trusting in the infallibility of the papacy, upon discovering its human, historical character, might one day awaken to realize that the category of infallibility is irrelevant to its practice of faith.

The principal truths which have traditionally guided us were derived from the creation story. When we were young, our parents and religion instructors taught us that God had created us, each and every one, for the sake of knowing, loving and serving God in this world, and of living with God forever in the next. Human beings owe their existence to God's deliberate choice to create the world, a decision which proceeded from love. This truth in no way was intended to preempt what we would eventually come to know about the world through cosmology, physics and astronomy. It had nothing to do with the age of the universe, or with its material origins, its physical composition, or the laws of nature which govern its evolution. Rather, this truth rested upon how the world showed itself; it drew its support from the human experience of the graciousness of life.

Life is a gift, and gifts are the expression of love, for love proves itself in deeds. The only fitting response to the awareness of how much we have been given is gratitude. The same love which called us into being would one day welcome us into eternity, to enjoy the definitive oneness with God which every human being inwardly craves. We want to love and to be loved; we want to embrace and to be embraced; we want to know and to be known. This desire is only partially realized in the course of our lives; for some unfortunate human beings, it is never realized at all. But to think about a union with each and every human being, with all of God's daughters and sons, in which we would simultaneously accept everyone and be accepted by everyone; to think about resting forever in the oneness of God is to suggest something which has the power to awaken hope even in the most desperate human life. This is the truth that we learned.

Of course, goodness is hardly the whole story. The same God who created the oceans and snow-capped mountains, which silence us with their awesome majesty, and who gave us both good foods to eat and the capacity to enjoy them, must also be responsible for the hideous cancers from which healthy people turn their faces, and the devastating droughts that leave millions of people thirsting and starving. Creation—our "mother" earth—delivers an uneven message about the gift-character of life. Life is good, when disease, injustice or nature itself do not stand in its way. The dark underbelly of creation can be deeply troubling for people trying to maintain their faith in God. Those who attack religious belief need only point to the obvious evils in the world to make the case for atheism, while those whose hold on faith is already tenuous easily stumble and fall when confronted with the menacing forces of destruction.

According to the Christian version of the creation story, human beings have been called into existence and loved. The same hand which first fashioned us in our mother's womb continues to create us until the moment when we shall step into that definitive oneness with the source of our life which we call the Spirit. Somewhere in the distant past, our ancestors in the faith reached a determination that the God who created the world is good, that creation is essentially good because God blessed it, and that even death is "good," provided it does not come prematurely. Death belonged to the divine plan for the world. In fact, belief in an afterlife appears relatively late in Israel's religious history; it was the Easter event that pushed Christians to look upon death as their passage to eternal life.

From the perspective of ordinary human experience, however, on either end of life, both in its origins and in its ultimate destiny, there is a great, wintry unknown. Our origins are presently shrouded within the obscure forces which brought the universe into existence, and our future is concealed by the veil of death. The biblical stories cannot change these facts; they simply make these great uncertainties manageable by placing God at the beginning and end of everything. As a result, we live within the stories, since we cannot find solace in the naked facts themselves. The only reality that we can be absolutely certain about is this world. If we could not appeal to the mystery of God in order to make sense of our existence, then what would happen to us? The landscape does turn pretty bleak when God is sliced out of the picture.

In order to defend ourselves against the chaos and uncertainty which assault our experience, we may resort to a faith which is "blind." We believe in God, we believe that God created us out of love, and we believe that one day God will take us into God's own self. We believe these things because we must; we believe because the alternative is unthinkable. In some sense, the alternative is intellectual and spiritual annihilation. At least so it appears to those of us who have been brought up believing in God. A world without God is meaningless, and so is human life.

Faith is not the soul's defense against the threat of intellectual and spiritual annihilation, however. It is not a leap of the mind in the face of unanswerable questions about the origins and final destiny of human beings, nor is it intended to supply for a shortfall in human knowledge about what is morally right and wrong. Faith does not say, "Let's pretend that there is a God so that we can sleep more securely at night," and prayer is not a lifelong conversation with an imaginary friend. Rather, faith renders the human person open to being completed or fully made by love. Indeed, from one point of view, faith might be regarded as our openness to being made more fully human. Love, compassion, wisdom won through suffering, forgiveness even of one's enemies, passion for the things of God: these reveal the full potential of our human nature. The person who lives by faith is saying, in effect, that we are made for love and we are made by love. That is what faith says; but what is its "reason"?

What was the basis of the determination which those first believers made about the goodness of the created world? Surely, they could not have been naive about the very real evil and hardship they had to endure in this world. They could have followed the route of other ancient peoples and concluded that there were two gods, one responsible for goodness and order, and the other responsible for evil and chaos. Or, with the Buddha, they could have pursued a noble path that transcends evil and suffering through meditation and wisdom. Apparently, they were seized by a different intuition. Out of that intuition they would reaffirm their conviction about God's goodness and faithfulness, even in the face of terrible personal and national tragedies. But why did they do this? Had they also realized that apart from such faith life would become even more desperate? In other words, was faith basically something negative, a protection against the unknown?

Once again, we cannot resolve this merely by appealing to the strength and example of those who have journeyed ahead of us. We do not live by their act of believing, but through our own. The intuition which grounded their act of faith in the divine creative goodness might, or might not, sustain us. It may be that the answer to whether goodness or evil will have the final say in a person's life will prove to be a toss-up. Some of us have experienced more goodness in life than evil. The subsequent intuition will thus be quantitative: goodness outweighs evil. I can imagine someone else, however, for whom life yields a very different sort of experience, one in which evil outweighs the good. What then?

One thing is clear. We cannot afford to be simplistic in matters of faith. As believers, we make assertions about God. But those assertions have to be grounded somewhere within experience in order for the act of faith to be accessible to those outside the community of belief, as well as to those who come on the scene in a later age. The reason many of us find the world to be a beautiful and friendly place may, in fact, have less to do with our belief about God than about the goodness of our parents, the security of our families, and the relative political and economic stability of our society. And once we have joined this experience to the church's assertion about God as loving creator, the grounding intuition becomes firm and complete. Given our backgrounds, it is relatively easy to assent to the proposition that we have been called into existence, each one of us personally, by love and for love. Still, how do we escape the gnawing suspicion that this intuition might contain a hidden, structural weakness?

If our lives during this time of transition are going to be guided by the truth, then it must be the whole truth about God and creation which must illumine our path, not a half-truth. The world which the creator blessed and pronounced good is at the same time a world where men and women have been choked to death by injustice, and where rewards and blessings have not been meted out equally. Either creation is not blessed, and the biblical story in Genesis has gotten things wrong, or else the tradition's introductory picture of God as creator is inexact and needs to sit in the developing pan of human experience a little longer.

The scriptural recognition of the earth's goodness has to be set alongside a recounting of human poverty and deprivation. "And God saw that it was good" from Genesis must be joined with "For the Lord loves justice" from the Psalms. The practical consequence of which for us would be, "Learn to do good; seek justice" (Isa 1:17). The same intuition which guides the eye from the beauty and goodness of the earth to the goodness and mercy of the creator, must also embrace the world's poverty, for the eye has to be guided from the wretchedness it sees to the throne of justice, and back.

The world does not send us mixed signals about the creator, provided we understand whose side God is on in the history of human suffering and oppression; but it does send us mixed signals about ourselves. Yet these mixed signals can direct us God-ward: the earth's goodness in a prayer of thanksgiving, and the earth's poverty in a prayer of protest and tears. Christian spirituality must build upon both of these realities if it wants to avoid naive romanticism about God, on the one hand, and unrelieved anger on the other. The first leads to the softness of untested faith, and the second leads to the hardness of commitment without love.

Christian truth is in transition because the historical experience out of which we read the great biblical stories has changed dramatically. Throughout the church men and women can no longer separate the stories of faith from the poverty, hunger and injustice endured by so many people. The truths of faith are anything but timeless: they are "timed" to the experience of men and women who hunger and thirst for God's justice. These truths are not meant to make us feel more secure at night because, as eternal verities, they shine down upon us from heaven to light our way. On the contrary, the truths that are going to guide us have been forged in the historical experience of people wandering and enduring; they glow from within a road paved by slavery and exile, exploitation and captivity, poverty and famine, the whim and the will of earthly powers. Such things may not be the markers of our experience, but they do mark the life stories of the vast majority of people. One of the things making this time of transition so uncomfortable is that we cannot reclaim the truths of our faith without being pulled into the experience of people on that hard road. Truth, like the Word, becomes flesh and blood; it takes on time and history, and clothes itself with the features of men and women heavily burdened, crying out to God for deliverance.

In a time of transition, the security traditionally associated with truth gives way to the uncertainty and expectation usually associated with hope. In the future, we may be guided more by the hopes of human beings who believe that the creator intended the good things of the earth for them, too, than by certitudes that would do little more than anchor privilege.

3

How Shall We Relate to God?

One of the limitations in the way that many of us conceive God is that we think of our relationship with God as one-on-one. We pray to God in the manner of a private conversation: we speak, God listens; God speaks, we listen. In that relationship, God can be imagined as the fixed point, the reliable, unchanging source of our being and life. Other people might come and go in our lives; they might change, they may even abandon us. Whatever disappointment their changing or their leaving may cause, at least we have the assurance that God will remain faithful and true. "All things are passing, God alone endures," wrote the sixteenth-century mystic, Teresa of Avila.

Conversation with God, however, is quite different from our conversations with one another. God never answers with audible sounds. At best, God's "speaking" is symbolic, and many times we are left trying to decipher what we suppose to be signs of God's presence and action in our lives. In most of our conversations with one another, topics emerge and fade. We question one another, argue, listen, and often tease something through together. The way we relate to God might be like the way a child speaks to an imaginary figure and we "talk things out," but then this usually amounts to little more than speaking out loud to oneself, even if the conversation is only taking place in our heads. Talking to God is not quite what it seems.

At those times when we really focus our attention on God, we may try to put into words what is transpiring in our hearts. The fact is, of course, that what we are thinking and feeling is already known to God before we ever utter a syllable, at least according to the biblical intuition about God:

37

> You know when I sit down and when I rise up;
>   you discern my thoughts from far away.
> Even before a word is on my tongue,
>   O Lord, you know it completely (Ps 139:2,4).

God is already aware of our sorrow, our gratitude, our joy, or our interior darkness, even before we speak, but the activity of praying frequently helps us to become reflectively aware of our inner state. Honest prayer, which is infinitely more than the mere recitation of formulas, creates an intimacy with life itself; we know life by tasting its moments. More importantly, however, the activity of praying is a way of consciously orienting ourselves toward the unseen but real foundation of our lives. And this happens no matter to whom we address our prayer: whether to Mary, or to one of the saints, or to Jesus. Although we may imagine ourselves talking to Jesus or to Mary, the intention of the heart really pierces the image we have in our minds and finds its center in God. This may have been what Paul had in mind when he wrote:

> Likewise the Spirit helps us in our weakness; for we do not know how to pray as we ought, but that very Spirit intercedes with sighs too deep for words. And God, who searches the heart, knows what is the mind of the Spirit, because the Spirit intercedes for the saints according to the will of God (Rom 8:26–27).

Ultimately, the activity of prayer transcends any of the imaging we may resort to, such as gospel scenes or episodes from the Old Testament. It also transcends any particular words we may utter or texts we may read. The reason is that what we are trying to say at any particular moment to God can only be essentially a variation on the basic prayer we are always making, namely, "I want you." This is true no matter what we are asking of God, or no matter what inner feeling we may be attempting to put into words. Our souls may be stirred to thankfulness, or to beg God's blessing and strength, or to express, in tears, our sorrow, or to cry, in outrage, for an end to poverty and injustice. Nevertheless, "I want you" is the quintessential prayer of the human heart; it is, when all is said and done, the heart's only prayer. It is what ties all the various movements of our souls together.

What each person needs to discover is that there is no approaching God alone. The reason is that while every human being is by virtue of his or her creation oriented toward God, every single human being is likewise oriented toward the rest of the human race. In the concluding chapter of her study on the Trinity, Catherine LaCugna writes:

> *Entering into divine life therefore is impossible unless we also enter into a life of love and communion with others.* . . . Living from others and for others is the path of glory in which we and God exist together. The light of God's grace and life can indeed be dimmed or possibly even extinguished by sin, which is the absence of praise and the annihilation of communion. The cardinal sin [is] the denial that we are persons from and for God, from and for others.[7]

For some writers, the doctrine of the Trinity provides the theological basis for the claim that there cannot be a private relationship with God. The God of Christian faith does not stand in a relationship to the world as one individual in isolation reaching out to another. Rather, divine life is already a communion; the "being" of God is to-be-in-relation. This means that the work of creation proceeds from communion and it remains incomplete until the human race is fully drawn into this life. Properly speaking, then, God does not create individuals; God creates the human community. Or rather, God creates men and women such that they are unfinished until they learn how to live together as brothers and sisters. God does not behold just "me"; God beholds "us." When each of us stands in God's sight, we stand there as people who want God. But the God our souls seek is a God who wants *us*, together. When it comes to Christian prayer, the heart of the matter is communion.

Needless to say, we need to be careful not to collapse the difference between God and us; the human race is not, and should never be regarded as, a substitute for God. Nevertheless, God has identified with us in a remarkable way. The *mystery* surrounding creation is not that it was God who fashioned the universe, but that God initiated a real relationship with creatures, a relationship which thereby makes them human. Yet this relationship needs a face, and the only face of God we shall ever behold in this life (and perhaps in the next) appears in the faces of our brothers and sisters. The nail print into which we put our finger, the wounded side into which we slide our hand, is none other than the human community with which Jesus is now everlastingly joined. Jesus has been crucified to the world, and the world to him, as Paul would have put it (Gal 6:14). The same holds true for all those who, like Jesus, have learned to live for others. The divine relationship with us is always routed through one another.

The way the classical Christian mystics talk about God could lead one to think that an individual, intimate relationship with God is the goal of Christian prayer and, indeed, of Christian life. Their experience of God appears to be all-absorbing and anything but an awareness of the connection between the divine life they seek and the human community of which they are a part. Yet there has to be another element even within the most intimate relationship with God, and one writer who called attention to it was Thomas Merton. In a celebrated passage from one of his journals, Merton wrote:

> In Louisville, at the corner of Fourth and Walnut, in the center of the shopping district, I was suddenly overwhelmed with the realization that I loved all those people, that they were mine and I theirs, that we could not be alien to one another even though we were total strangers. It was like walking from a dream of separateness, of spurious self-isolation in a special world . . . The whole illusion of a separate holy existence is a dream.[8]

To be fair, it must be said that those who belonged to the classical mystical tradition did not share twentieth-century social consciousness, nor did they possess the categories or conceptual tools to analyze their experience the way we might do it today. Still, the sense of privacy lingers over their experience of God, even when that experience impelled them to devote themselves unreservedly and heroically to serving their neighbors, and that same sense of privacy often hangs over our experience as well. But in this passage, Merton appears to have undergone a breakthrough in his awareness of the mystery of God. The divine mystery and presence are inseparable from human beings. While these are truly distinct realities, we have to add that we never enter God's presence alone, because God never "sees" or "hears" us alone, either.

Although prayer is often loosely described as our talking to God, I believe that talking to God in the sense most people envision it does not make sense. I recall several occasions when good people confided that they neither prayed nor believed in God; they were professed religious. That they did not believe in God I could understand, because for many Christians God has been reduced to an object. Like the God of many scientists, *that* God of popular piety rightfully can be said not to exist. That they did not pray intrigued me, because I do not see how intelligent people could not pray. By praying I mean a lived orientation to the heart's desire, which is Love itself. How can any human being who is sincerely trying to become more human not act out, in thought and in deed, this orientation toward the hidden ground of all love and desire?

The definition of prayer which they were rejecting is one modeled after the way human beings speak with one another. As we noted earlier, God cannot be pulled into human language this way. Why does prayer in church so frequently sound like a valiant effort to inform God of something? Or are such prayers crafted as a roundabout way of reminding congregations that they must acknowledge their dependence upon God, or that they must work for peace, or that they must learn not to take the blessings they have received for granted? Are these prayers aimed at God, or are they actually directed to us?

In truly liberated praying, the human intention always goes beyond the words we use to express ourselves, and therein lies the real prayer, the desire which runs "too deep for words." Perhaps it could be argued that, in a similar way, the neighbor is always "there" when we place ourselves in God's presence, even though we may not be thinking of him. For the fact is that God does see him, too; God does hear her: the brother or sister, indeed, all the brothers and sisters who make up the human race. The more we bring this basic fact to explicit awareness, the more disposed we shall be to hear whatever it is that God wants to "speak" to us.

4

Prayer in a Time of Transition

The notion of transition implies a "not." For example, if I am in transition, then I am no longer in the place I was yesterday; I am here. If I remain in a state of transition, then tomorrow I will not be here; I shall be somewhere else.

Transition does not connote the same thing as journeying or pilgrimage. To conceive one's life as a journey or as a pilgrimage is to impose meaning and purpose on whatever happens. Like the two disciples on the road to Emmaus, we look for and discover the meaningfulness of the things that happened to us "on the way." The importance of chance encounters, accidents, remembrances, decisions and relationships is always relative to the journey itself. If we describe ourselves as pilgrims or sojourners in this world, then that tells people something about us. It tells them that we do not consider our true homeland to be here. Thus, we have to concentrate the energies of our soul on making our way through this present existence.

Transition and pilgrimage, then, name different ways of experiencing the world. And although it has often been a highly attractive religious metaphor for many people, the journey motif does not account for all the elements of our experience. It ties many of them together, but not all, because the journey metaphor leaves the soul divided: how much of ourselves should we invest in this world, if the truth is that we are merely walking through? There are even some people who tremble at the thought of committing themselves to practically anything serious or long-range. The idea of being on a journey may appeal to a basic insecurity about life and legitimize their unwillingness to make a promise. The prospect of always being on a journey can be a false road to freedom, especially when it leads us to tie up the tendrils of our souls so that they cannot fall into the world of the poor.

Yet all of us share the experience of passing through different stages or periods of human life as we grow older. Life's great "passages" are concerned with psychological growth and emotional or affective development; each stage of our lives calls attention both to life's *not* and to its *not yet*. This "not," which is central to the experience of being in transition, can be purifying and cleansing, if we do not resist it. The way we pray and relate to God as a fifty-year-old should be different from the way a child prays and thinks about God, if we have been at all serious throughout our lives about practicing our faith. There are some Christian adults, however, who keep trying to pray and relate to God the same way they did as youngsters, even when the older prayer forms or ways of thinking have ceased to be effective. They worked once; why shouldn't they work for us now? It does not occur to them that it is the Spirit, and not the council or some theological "expert," that has been drawing them into uncharted territory.

As we move through life, and respond to its invitations to become ever more adult, ever more free, we will necessarily be separated from things and relationships which are not essential to our well-being. We surpass the level of development of the former self as we become more liberated from our anxieties and fears, more in touch with the springs of life within us. Paul referred to this in expressions like "putting on Christ" (Rom 13:14) and becoming a "new creation" (2 Cor 5:17). Furthermore, just as individuals pass through moments of transition, so do communities and whole societies.

The gospel warns us that it is as perilous for groups, as it is for individuals, to resist the Spirit and fail to discern the signs of the times:

> He answered them, "When it is evening, you say, 'It will be fair weather, for the sky is red.' And in the morning, 'It will be stormy today, for the sky is red and threatening.' You know how to interpret the appearance of the sky, but you cannot interpret the signs of the times" (Mt 16:2–3).

Transition is a sign of our times. It reveals the "not" which is part and parcel of human existence itself; it is revealed in the awareness that we

What is God's name? (handwritten annotation at top)

are not yet fully of God. Until the moment when one can say, "The Spirit and I are one," then the *not*—the incompleteness—of our existence will continue to manifest itself. We are not yet the fully liberated men and women God intends us to be, and justice does not yet reign on the earth.

To talk about God in a time of transition is actually to echo what many spiritual writers have long pointed out. After asking whether human language is capable of expressing what God is, Thomas Aquinas answered: "such words do say something of what God is, though inadequately, because we can only talk of God as we know him, and we know him only through creatures, which represent him inadequately."[9] Yet maybe here the so-called "negative" (sometimes referred to as "apophatic") tradition of prayer may be closer to Christian experience than the "positive" (or "kataphatic") tradition which Thomas is defending. The divine mystery is known "better" (if we can qualify our knowledge of God this way) negatively than positively because it is easier to affirm what God is not, rather than what God is:

(handwritten margin note: Aquinas our knowing of God is inadequate)

> To think God is unavoidably to think the name of God. But what *is* God's name? What does *God* name? How does *God* name? Does *God* name? Perhaps . . . *God* is the name that makes the disappearance of the name—every name—appear. If this is so, *God* is *in a certain sense* a name for the unnameable. . . . To learn to think God is to learn how not to think God.[10] *Mark Taylor* (handwritten)

This is not simply an admission of the limitations of all our language about God. The issue is not language; it is the divine mystery itself. The limitations involved in speaking about God arise because of the nature of our experience of the divine mystery, and behind our experience there lies the nature of God's becoming known to us. Thus it is sometimes characteristic of the Spirit, as our contemplative abilities develop, to wean us away from images and pictures, even from the familiar and consoling images we might have treasured of Jesus. An anonymous writer from the fourteenth century observed:

> For in the beginning it is usual to feel nothing but a kind of darkness about your mind, as it were, *a cloud of unknowing.* You

(handwritten margin note: Cloud of Unknowing)

will seem to know nothing and to feel nothing except a naked intent toward God in the depths of your being. Try as you might, this darkness and cloud will remain between you and your God. You will feel frustrated, for your mind will be unable to grasp him, and your heart will not relish the delight of his love. But learn to be at home in this darkness. . . . For if, in this life, you hope to feel and see God as he is in himself it must be within this darkness and this cloud. [11]

The writer has experienced God in darkness, under a "cloud of unknowing," because such is the very nature of God's self-revelation. God cannot be identified purely and simply with any created thing, not even with the human features of Jesus. *Then why Jesus?*

As an example of the experience our fourteenth-century author might have been trying to describe we could turn to the story of Elijah:

He said, "Go out on and stand on the mountain before the Lord, for the Lord is about to pass by." Now there was a great wind, so strong that it was splitting mountains and breaking rocks in pieces before the Lord, but the Lord was not in the wind; and after the wind an earthquake, but the Lord was not in the earthquake; and after the earthquake a fire, but the Lord was not in the fire; and after the fire a sound of sheer silence" (1 Kings 19:11–12).

God, we are told, was going to "pass by," almost as if such passing by should be a familiar characteristic of the way the divine mystery is revealed to human beings. God appears in the passing; God speaks while moving. A residential, stationary or immovable God would be uncharacteristic of Israel's experience. The God who is about to speak to Elijah is not in the earthquake, not in the fire, not in the wind storm. Nor, we might add, is God to be found in the stars, or in the oceans, or even in the grandeur of the earth.

God appears *in* the transition. God is revealed in the middle of all that is passing precisely as the *not* of our existence: God is *not* in the fire, or in the earthquake. In other words, God is *not* to be identified with nature's displays of power, or, if we read "fire," "wind" and "earthquake" as metaphors, God is certainly *not* to be identified with any of the stormy forces, political events, and social upheavals which characterize our time. No one can simply assert, "See, this is the result of God's anger or displeasure." Wars, tragedies, famines and epidemics are never divine punishments, and they ought never to be confused with God's word: they are not the sort of words God uses to draw us closer to himself, or to chastise us, or to teach us patience. By the same token, we cannot facilely assume that a nation's political and scientific triumphs, or abundant harvests, or the possession of a long life or a healthy body, are messages of divine approval. Neither are these things the words which God uses to address us. All such assumptions must pass under the cloud of unknowing.

At the same time, God is always "there" for us; but God is there, so to speak, in that "sound of sheer silence" which calls attention to what God is not. The negativity which we experience as we pass through our time and place, the sense of letting go and of leaving things behind; the erosion of certitudes; the disorienting prospect that not only did the older forms of our religiousness not bring us any closer to God than the disappointing forms of today (since there is no way we can force God to be present to us through liturgical actions, or devotional practices, or religious art), but also that genuine knowledge of God may lie in a totally different direction from the path in which one has been accustomed to search for God, namely, through "private" prayer: all this helps to describe what believing people today are passing through.

Prayer during major historical moments of transition and interior disorientation, of confusion and of leaving the familiar behind, cannot afford to be anything but simple and direct: a prayer purely from the heart. Tried and true formulas will no longer work, because, as we said, the divine presence cannot be summoned through a formula, no matter how sacred. Images and rites that we depended upon in the childhood of our faith must give way to something new. What this newness is going to consist of remains to be seen. For now, all we can do is endeavor to discern the signs of our times, to ponder what is happening around us. Strong currents are pulling the community of faith; but to where?

5

The Need for a New Aesthetic

In moments of transition, as change breaks the spell which old certainties and familiar patterns held over us, we may well experience God as curiously distant, even missing from the world. It is like passing the house where a close friend once lived: the building is still there, the neighborhood appears the same, but a feeling of emptiness hangs in the air as memory recalls the laughter and love shared with the one who once lived there.

As we just saw, a major ingredient of this experience can be accounted for by recalling the "not" which lies at the very heart of the way we approach God through language, symbols and concepts. God cannot be contained by the vocabulary we have at our disposal, or forced to appear through rites and ceremonies, or enclosed within sacred texts or sacred space. In moments of transition the truth about God's freedom and transcendence becomes painfully clear. If we attempt going back over the well-traveled roads, we may find that the divine presence has long since moved on.

One other experience which can trigger our awareness of this "not" is the experience of suffering, particularly suffering which is undeserved. Some pain we bring on ourselves, and of that we ought not complain too loudly; but what of the misery which is unjust? What about people forced to flee their homes because of war or famine? What about those persecuted because they belong to an ethnic or religious minority? What about those whose labor has been grossly and systematically exploited? What of the countless thousands of those who disappeared in the hands of military governments?

Religious people have wrestled long and hard with the tension between their belief in divine goodness and their experience of a flawed, unfair world. They have puzzled over why the unrighteous appear to thrive, while the poor and victimized struggle for the most meager share of this world's goods. Virtuous living is not automatically rewarded, and villainous living goes unevenly punished. And when the villains are pulled down from their thrones, sometimes they land squarely on the fragile dwellings of the poor. To adapt a gospel text, the last state of a people can be worst than the first (Lk 11:26). This unfairness similarly reveals more about what God is not than what God is, because the God of our tradition is supposed to be a God of justice and compassion.

The distance we perceive between the world as we find it and the world as we conceive God to have intended it brings us once more to the "not" within our experience. "This is not it," our eyes keep assuring us. "This is not the way the world ought to be." The presence of evil in the world, especially the unequal distribution of this world's goods, creates a sense of distance between us and God. On the one hand, our religious instinct says, God could not have anything to do with injustice and oppression: these things cannot be of God. Yet on the other hand, God clearly determined that human beings should spend their lives here. Thus we live across a divide, separated from our idea of God by the reality of oppression and poverty. And no amount of theological bridge-building seems to have helped; God and evil cannot be harmonized, whether we are dealing with the misfortune of whole peoples, or whether we are dealing with the pain and tragedy which afflict individual lives. The result: God feels distant, even alien to human concerns.

Karl Rahner expressed some of the same sentiments in different words. After describing the distance from God which many people today have experienced, Rahner wrote:

> God's distance means that our spirit has become humble in the face of an insoluble puzzle. It means that our heart is despondent over unanswered prayers, and is tempted to look on "God" only as one of those grand and ultimately unbelieved-in words under cover of which people hide their despair, because this despair no longer has the power to accept even itself as real. God seems to us to be only that unreal, inaccessible infinity which, to our torment, makes our tiny bit of reality seem still more finite and questionable.

This infinity makes us seem homeless even in *our* world, because it leads us to the extravagance of a yearning that we can never fulfill, and that even he does not seem to fulfill.

Yes, it appears that contemporary Western humankind, more than the people of earlier times, must mature expiatingly in the purgatory of this distance from God. If in the destiny of individuals it happens that besides the blessed day of the near God, there is the night of the senses and of the spirit, in which the infinity of the living God comes nearer to human beings by seeming to be more distant and not at all near, why should such times not also be experienced in the destiny of nations and continents?[12]

The way many of us relate to God has been conditioned by at least two things, although we may not be aware of the depth of their influence. First, there is the culture around us, and the feature of that culture which has perhaps played the biggest part in the way we construct our relation to God is its individualism. Society forms and educates us to think, choose and act in terms of what is best for the individual, rather than what will advance the good of the whole. Education is thus geared to enhancing personal careers and "maximizing" one's potential for success. Morality becomes a fundamentally individualistic and private matter. Our preferred mode of transportation is private. Our approach to ownership is private. We tend to pursue private or individual interests before the public good, which freezes every effort to meet national and global problems in its tracks. Rugged independence turns into a sort of national virtue. Even devout, righteous people can stand before God as if what mattered most in God's sight was their private virtue with respect to God's law. What was reprehensible about the Pharisee's attitude as he stood praying in the Temple was not his boasting of his piety, nor even the implication that he did not really need God's mercy; rather, it was that he believed that the only thing which mattered in his relationship to God was the status of his individual salvation or justification. It was not his pride that kept him unjustified, but his daring to stand alone, as if he could step away from the sinful human community to which he really belonged, although he would never have been able to admit this.

the aura of the sacred in church

The second thing which has conditioned the way we have related to God is what I would call (for want of a better term) a religious aesthetic. By this I mean a sensibility or attitude toward the world and the historical experience of human beings which leads us to construe certain parts of reality in terms of God. The imagination develops the habit of picking up a divine resonance within things, or of associating certain things with God. I am not always altogether sure what "God" means for people; the word may signify no more than some vague feeling of security in the face of the vastness of a universe whose origins are beyond the mind's reach. Or it may refer to the Word made flesh, casting a holy transparency over all creation. Whatever the case, certain things have come to be associated with the divine and contribute to creating a distinctive, "spiritual" mood: the dark chapel, the stained glass, the lingering scent of incense, the glow of the vigil lights, the liturgical chants, the mystique of the liturgy itself, the veiled tabernacle, statues and icons, holy books, relics of the saints. These may also have enabled us to feel as if we had come into contact with God, although the traditional religious aesthetic does not generally transfer to life outside the sanctuary. The aura of the sacred may hang in the air for a while outside our places of worship, but within a short time it evaporates unnoticed amidst the preoccupations of the profane world.

Even the so-called "proofs" or "arguments" for the existence of God, which received their classical formulation under the pen of Thomas Aquinas, ultimately appeal to some aesthetic sense about the goodness and order of the universe: Of course it is only reasonable to assume the existence of a creator who is both intelligent and good, given the intelligibility and goodness of the visible world! But what about people whose basic outlook on life is chaotic and painful, who discern neither order nor goodness around them? For people such as these, the classical arguments become much harder to embrace, because the arguments presuppose a view of reality which they would find implausible. They might very well believe in God, but not on the basis of the universe's well-ordered design and goodness.

Still, there is no doubt that things of beauty have the power to move us; there is no doubt, too, that religious art forms, like art in general, mediate an aesthetic experience which can be truly uplifting and ennobling. All created things, in fact, have this potential, since all created things are manifestations of divine artistry. Nevertheless, an aesthetic experience is not in itself an experience of God, and it would be a mistake to confuse the two.

Today we desperately need a new religious aesthetic. We need a new way of looking at ourselves and our world which can mediate for us a sense of the presence of God in our midst, a guiding intuition which would inform our religious sensibilities but does not stop at the church door. This aesthetic must be able to make us ever more critically aware of the individualism which our culture promotes, with its exaggerated sense of private ownership and personal fulfillment. Yet this intuition cannot be merely invented or dreamt up; it has to originate in the signs of the times. The old aesthetic forms expressed the genius (and perhaps the longings) of another time and place. The melodies of the Gregorian chants, which I found immensely moving for a number of years, breathed life into the still, barren walls of the chapel I used to pray in. The old order of the mass, together with the liturgical gestures of the priest as he recited the prayers in hushed tones, transported me into a world apart, reassuringly distinct from everything else. But essentially those forms worked by drawing the heart toward heaven, not toward the earth, and the breath that was blown was a sigh for eternity.

Those men and women who do not share the impulse that wants to erect temples and cathedrals, those who wonder whether our current forms of worship will ever succeed in putting us in touch with the elementary pieces of our human experience today, may be prepared to agree that the mystery of God appears in the *not*: *not* in the building and its sturdy granite walls, *not* in the sacred music, *not* in the liturgy's dramatic forms, *not* in the stained glass or in the paintings and images of Christ and the saints, and *not* in the intuition about holiness which once lay behind these things. For them, the mystery of God must be associated with something else. Imagination needs to develop a different habit.

I have met many young people who, once inside a church, do not have the faintest notion of what the eucharistic liturgy is all about. If the eucharist is supposed to bear some resemblance to a meal, the building certainly bears little resemblance to a place where men and women might gather to eat. They grasp the purpose served by the

3 reasons for spiritual disengagement ↓

readings and the homily, but after these they are at a loss. Even once the form and meaning of the eucharist are explained, they remain unmoved and spiritually disengaged, despite their most sincere efforts. As I see it, there are at least three reasons for what has happened. First, they do not know the full story of Jesus, and thus the eucharist is not firmly connected to the gospel memories about him. Second, while they are more than willing to assume roles in the liturgy, such as servers, lectors, singers and eucharistic ministers, the net effect of what they do at the liturgy does not yield a renewed sense of the presence of God in our world. And thirdly, the aesthetic forms of which the eucharistic liturgy is constructed—its prayers, its music, the vestments worn by the priest, its sacred space, and so on—bear little relevance to our time and place within history. One does not adore food, for example; one eats it. Over the centuries, eucharistic piety succumbed to the human tendency to sacralize things and concentrate the divine mystery in a blessed object: the bread and cup were declared to be Christ in a way that many people today can neither comprehend nor accept. The fact that so many young people cannot relate meaningfully to the principal Christian ritual is a sign of our times, too; indeed, it is symptomatic of a tragic rupture between experience and faith.

Where, then, shall we search in an effort to develop a new aesthetic, a contemporary sense of the presence of God? With what shall we learn to associate the divine mystery? What sights, sounds or objects will evoke in us today an awareness of God's presence among us and *God's abiding interest in this world*? What themes and desires will inform our music, our symbols and rituals, and religious art, and what concerns will awaken once again the powerful and "dangerous" memory of Jesus' life? And since the liturgical prayers are designed to center our attention rather than God's, what realities do we need to keep constantly before our awareness?

There has been a marked tendency over the centuries to connect the celebration of the eucharist with the "heavenly liturgy" which serves as a symbolic backdrop in the letter to the Hebrews. The eye of the church at prayer frequently falls on Christ in glory. But should not the liturgy be directed toward the earth instead of toward the heavens, since this is where we have to live and *this is where we have to find God?* It is into this world that we pray for the kingdom of God to come.

Instead of celebrating the power of an "Almighty God and Father" who reigns on high, or instead of celebrating the victory of the Lamb of God who has taken away the sins of the world, perhaps we need to start with the reality of human beings in this world and ask, "How can their experience (and ours) be read and transformed in light of the gospel story?" What are the key elements within that experience which need to be set in relief?

Mindfulness of the Poor and the Oppressed

Over the past twenty years or so, a new aesthetic has in fact been forming, and it is gradually reshaping our consciousness of what it means to be church. The Christian imagination has become increasingly sensitized to God's preferential love for the poor. It is developing the habit of seeing "God" wherever it finds human beings impoverished and oppressed, terrorized and homeless. Gradually it is digesting the fact that the salvation of the few is going to depend upon the liberation of the many; in other words, salvation is impossible apart from our solidarity with the poor. By joining our aspirations with theirs, and by passing over as much as is humanly possible into the world of their deprivation, we are cultivating a renewed Christian sensitivity to the presence of God in our world.

The prayers we compose and the music we sing need increasingly to reflect the suffering and hope of the poor, because in a particular way the God of Jesus is among them in their history, in their present experience and in their aspirations. How shall we lift our hearts in song to the Lord, if the songs we sing take little account of the impoverished reality of most men and women of our age? Shall we praise and glorify the Lord, but never cry out our protest against the wretchedness which prevails in so many lives? Will the piety of western Christians who have come of age forever be the piety of men and women who have no contact with the lives of those who struggle? A revolutionary hymn now and then might do us a world of good.

I do not want to suggest that God is unconcerned about the rest of us, especially in our moments of severe pain, or temptation and inner struggle, or heartfelt thankfulness. But just as a parent would find it hard to be fully attentive to a child who was complaining about a broken toy while his sister was fighting for her life in a hospital bed, perhaps so also God. And just as parents would try to help all their children to learn to think and love as a family, so too God works to create such mindfulness in us. The reign of God is always going to require more of us because, on balance, more has been given to us.

Any Christian assembly which has not even occasional contact with the experience of economically, socially and politically disadvantaged people of today, and which is not in principle open to their presence but remains unmindful of their needs and their cries, may find itself in the position of the child clamoring for the attention of a preoccupied parent. Their liturgical worship is going to reveal itself to be increasingly disconnected from the world and from history, which is what happens when worship is dissociated from the story of Jesus. The grand work of redemption which is mentioned so often in our sacramental worship is rendered vacuous unless we see the connection between the life and death of Jesus, and the life and death of those in the world who hunger and thirst for justice.

To be a person necessarily means that we are in relationship with others. Being a person is fundamentally relational, and social. Human beings in relation constitute a society. The Christian notion of God grasps this point extremely well. For if God is personal, then the being of God, too, has to be relational. Thus we speak about a communion of three "persons" in one God.

But this notion of God as personal, and thus as being in relation, affects the way God figures into our life. God cannot function as a fixed, unchanging point, and still remain the God who passes, even though the Psalmist depicts God as a "rock" and a "mighty fortress." This also holds true for human beings, since to be a human being is to be in the process of creation and constantly to be passing over into something new. No one who is open to life can remain the same forever, because we are always growing, always undergoing conversion and renewal, always enlarging our capacity for compassion, wisdom and love.

Yet there is also another reason why we cannot remain the same. Who we are, and how we develop, is very much a function of the people around us and the events of our times. Thus, we are not only developing; we are also becoming increasingly social. We are daily becoming men and women ever more conscious of our world. Furthermore, that world itself is constantly growing: we know more about it, the economies and political fortunes of nations are becoming increasingly interdependent, its sad and sorry stories appear nightly on our television screens. The world which we share with other human beings and its concerns figure into our evolving awareness of who we are; they reshape the way we think of ourselves. All men and women somehow belong to us, and we to them.

For a Christian, this point should be almost self-evident. To grow in the Spirit involves our understanding ever more radically and profoundly what it means to belong to the whole people of God. Today in a dramatic way the poor reveal the *not* of God. For while God has identified with them through the history of Israel and the story of Jesus, it must be said that poverty, famine and injustice are not of God. More than anything else, the poor constantly testify to the great truth that God is better known through what God is not.

If the way we think about God assumes at the outset that we exist in a one-to-one relationship with God, then we have already allowed a mistake to slip into our thinking. There is nothing individualistic about a person's relationship with God because to be in relation with God is automatically to be in relation with all the other men and women, both living and dead, with whom God is in relation.

But the gospels recall that Jesus addressed God as Father. Does this not suggest that Jesus' relationship with God was personal in the way that any son or daughter would relate to a mother or father? The objection is a good one; the Christian experience of God is rightly called "personal." As Rahner, voicing over Ignatius, confessed: "All I say is I knew God, nameless and unfathomable, silent and yet near, bestowing himself upon me in his Trinity, I knew God beyond all concrete imaginings. I knew Him clearly in such nearness and grace as is impossible to confound or mistake." How is it, therefore, that our relationship with this God is not one-to-one?

The answer is that our relationship to God, as Rahner noted, always transcends every concrete imagining. That is true for us; it would also have been true for Jesus. Even the title "Father" names inadequately the full nature of the divine mystery. The God whom we address remains a God who has shared the divine image and likeness with all men and women. The God who "created the heavens and the earth" has seen fit to dwell in every human heart, even the hearts of the most wretched among us. Each time we pronounce the word "God," therefore, the soul is reaching out horizontally, as it were, into the human community past and present (for God is a God of the living: all are alive to him [Lk 20:38]). It reaches out, however unconsciously, to the One who is a God of and for persons. Just as God does not behold only me, but at the same time always and everywhere beholds the faces of all men and women, so also when we turn to God we wind up facing all of our brothers and sisters. To look at God, in other words, is to approach the world with a transformed vision. To be with God in prayer is always to be with the entire world, for it has not pleased God to allow us to see him "alone."

PART TWO
WHERE SHALL WE LOOK
FOR JESUS?

1

Not Among the Dead,
But Among the Living

The fourth gospel tells the story of Mary Magdalene's encountering two angels at the empty tomb of Jesus:

> They said to her, "Woman, why are you weeping?" She said to them, "They have taken away my Lord, and we do not know where they have laid him" (Jn 20:13).

When the risen Jesus addressed her, she mistook him for the gardener who tended the burial site:

> "Sir, if you have carried him away, tell me where you have laid him, and I will take him away" (20:15).

As soon as he spoke her name, Mary recognized that it was indeed Jesus, and she reached out to grab hold of him. But Jesus would not allow her to do so:

> "Do not hold on to me, because I have not yet ascended to the Father" (20:17).

This symbolic episode reveals several interesting elements about John's understanding of the status of the risen Jesus as well as the believer's experience of him. One feature is that the risen Jesus does not appear the way he used to, before his death and burial. He has taken on, apparently, different features; in one of Luke's stories, the disciples even believe they have been confronted by a ghost (Lk 24:37)!

Another feature is that the new place of the risen Jesus is with the Father, that is, in a definitive union with God. Any effort to prevent Jesus from reaching that oneness with God, no matter how well-intentioned, runs contrary to the real meaning of the story. Clearly, Jesus does not identify himself with God; otherwise his words, "I am ascending to my Father and your Father, to my God and your God" (20:17) would make no sense. At the same time, the one who would look for Jesus from now on must seek the Father.

In terms of the believer's experience of Jesus risen, there are also several intriguing features. First, there is what we might call the "pre-moment" of uncertainty. Although Mary is the only person mentioned, she is clearly not alone ("and *we* do not know where they have laid him"). It may be that in this case, Mary Magdalene thus represents a group of believers. Her experience and reaction to the outcome of the Jesus story would not be unique. Mary assumes that some unidentified people have removed the body of Jesus. The gospel writer does not exactly explain why Mary came to the tomb (Luke, for example, tells us that several women came to the tomb with spices to anoint the body of Jesus, since there had not been time to do so earlier). But the fourth gospel leaves us room to wonder. Perhaps Mary (and presumably her companions) simply came to the tomb out of grief, to mourn the death of one whom they loved. Loss and uncertainty would naturally have been two key elements of their experience.

After discovering that the tomb was empty, Mary rushed to fetch Peter and the beloved disciple. They raced to the site, verified her account, and then "returned to their homes." Did her original companions leave also? The following encounter with Jesus risen suggests that this is a "private" appearance of Jesus risen to Mary Magdalene; but it is not impossible that her companions remained with her, and that although Jesus spoke with Mary, her experience was a collective or communal one. Mary would thus represent a class of believers.

A second intriguing feature is that Mary's initial impulse is to cling to Jesus, but Jesus will not allow this. Perhaps the evangelist is thereby teaching us that faith cannot terminate in Jesus; it must go one step farther and recognize the oneness Jesus now has with God. The familiar characteristics of the human Jesus have to be set aside, passed over, or left under a cloud of unknowing. Mary, as a representative believer, has just discovered that her faith in Jesus lies in transition. What once was can no longer be. Any attempt to keep things the way they were is bound to meet with frustration, because Jesus exists no longer in the older forms. They are empty. His "real" presence lies elsewhere, wherever men and women find God, or wherever the divine mystery chooses to reveal itself to them.

This part of the story, we can imagine, must have been painful for one who had loved Jesus so much. "They have taken away my Lord" expresses her sense of loss; "I do not know where they have laid him" voices her sense of confusion about where she must now search to find Jesus.

The words "He is not here, but has risen" (Luke 24:5b) are somewhat unhelpful, because the meaning of "risen" is not at all so clear as we might guess. What does it mean to be "risen"? Does it simply mean "in heaven"? Or does "risen" refer to something altogether new and different, beyond one's wildest expectations? Does "risen" mean constantly "going ahead" of his companions (Mk 16:7), to prepare a new future? Does "risen" imply always going beyond what is in order to create the possibility for what might be?

Or is "risen" another way of talking about the great "not" of our experience: "He is *not here*"? For in addition to meaning that Jesus is no longer in the tomb, the messenger's statement describes a permanent feature of Christian experience. "Jesus is not *here*," because "here" denotes what is passing. Thus the question, "Why do you look for the living among the dead?" (Lk 24:5) assumes a deeper level of meaning. The question which the messengers put to the women can be directed to believers of every generation; certainly, it can be addressed to us in a time of transition. Why look for the risen One within lifeless forms, or within bloodless ideas, or within decaying institutions, or within the all-too-familiar categories of the past? To cling to such things would amount to imprisoning faith within a Galilean fantasy rather than releasing it to embrace the future and even the whole world. Why deify Jesus, which Mary seems to be attempting to do? To do this, even for love, would cause faith *in God* to stall, because it would attempt to capture Jesus before he had completed his ascent to the Father.

Jesus is not fully himself until he is finally one with the Father who sent him, and the same must hold true for each of us, with one qualification. Our becoming fully ourselves, the way Jesus was fully himself, does not occur apart from the Spirit of Jesus, which is always the Father's gift. Being fully oneself does not occur until one has first fully "emptied himself" (Phil 2:7) through love and service of one's sisters and brothers. The Father poured the Spirit into Jesus at his baptism, and the Father also pours the very same Spirit which enabled Jesus to "empty himself" and live for others into us.

Mary Magdalene's impulse to cling to Jesus is understandable; she wanted him back. The evangelist's corrective is likewise understandable: do not cling to what cannot be. Maybe the evangelist was trying to wean Christians who had not known Jesus away from some romantic desire to return to the days when Jesus actually lived. Such a correction would make sense, of course, because we cannot live in a false world, nor can we can we keep sighing, "If only I had been alive then, to walk with the disciples and to listen to Jesus!"

Yet stressing Jesus' oneness with the Father, his ascension and definitive departure from this world at the expense of the story is not very helpful, either. The imagination needs to know something about the one whom it wants to follow; it needs to relive or reenact the key moments of the gospel story. Human salvation does not work itself out in the abstract, but within history. To concentrate on Jesus' ascension to the Father without knowing the story which preceded that moment would be to make Christian faith into a religion of pure mysticism. If the fourth gospel were the only gospel available to us, then this would become a real danger.

We can view the episode at the tomb another way, however. The point here is not that we should not cling to the story of Jesus, or that we should forbid our imagination from wanting to immerse itself in the world of that story in order to "walk" with Jesus and his companions. But clinging to Jesus in a way that wants to hold him for oneself, or to preserve a private relationship with him, simply will not work. The grave site is not a place to look for him, or to keep him. Jesus is always with the living, that is, he is with men and women who thirst for the reign of God, and thus it is to them that one must go. The ascension probably ought to be imagined horizontally (into the world), not vertically (into the heavens). At all costs we cling to the story, because to lose the story would be to lose all sense of what Jesus means to our history. The oneness Jesus now enjoys with the Father ought not to be conceived in private terms, either. Even Jesus cannot make God into his private possession. The Father is the God of all, and certainly not just the God of Jesus. For us, as for Jesus, oneness with God automatically spells solidarity with God's people, the vast majority of whom are poor. We must allow him, therefore, to "ascend" to God, because through this "ascension" Jesus draws his disciples with him firmly into the heart of the world.

2

Reading the Gospel Story
Like Adults

The first major breakthrough in our religious lives may be the moment when we discover the humanity of Jesus. The second major breakthrough occurs when, with and through Jesus, we encounter the God of Jesus' faith. The first discovery gives rise to a way of living radically centered on Jesus as someone to whose experience we can relate, because he is like us in all things. The second discovery invites us to look beyond the purpose and mission of Jesus' life in order to know the God who called him and, through the proclaiming of his story, calls us.

For most of us, the basic claim of Christian faith concerns the divine status of Jesus. Our introduction to the gospel story centered around Christmas: the child who was born in Bethlehem under the humblest of circumstances is none other than the eternal Son of God. Although we knew (theoretically, at least) that the person of Jesus was not the same as the Father, for all practical purposes Jesus functioned in our religious lives as God. He possessed the same divine qualities which we believed belonged to God: all powerful, all knowing, all present, all loving. Usually, it was through those qualities that we related to him in our prayer and in our imagination.

But a fundamental problem, submerged under alternating layers of doctrine and devotion, eventually breaks through to the surface. For those who listen to the gospels carefully, the divine Jesus, or the Christ of the church's faith, does not exhibit those same divine qualities in the course of the gospel stories. The more we learn about how the gospels were composed, together with the social and historical conditions in which they were written, the more do we see the difference between the actual story of Jesus and what the church eventually came to believe about him. Oftentimes, individual episodes within the gospels reveal a great deal about the situation of the early church four or five decades after the death of Jesus. Sometimes Jesus is portrayed as making claims about himself, for example, which Jesus himself would never have made. Sometimes the evangelists have inserted Jesus into conflict situations which reflect the circumstances in Palestine years after Jesus' death. A number of the controversies reported in the fourth gospel, for instance, are based on tensions which later erupted between the Christian community and the larger Jewish community, yet Jesus is painted into those controversies as if he had actually been present.

Some people might be bothered by such disclosures. But the fact of the matter is that the story of Jesus would mean nothing to us, if it were divorced from our faith in and about him. Or perhaps a more accurate way to state this would be that the actual story of Jesus becomes significant to us only at the point in which we hear it as a story about God. I do not mean that we have to identify Jesus with God in order for the story to grab our attention. I mean that apart from Jesus' own faith in God (and the faith of the people of Israel from whom he comes), the actual history of Jesus would have little relevance to anyone's life. Above all, Jesus was utterly convinced that the reign of God was about to come. Jesus believed, absolutely, in the power and presence of God; the God of Israel was a God involved in human history. Jesus also believed, completely and unreservedly, that the God of Israel desired justice, and that this God had a special concern and affection for the poor and the powerless.

In short, the gospels disclose two levels of faith: the faith of Jesus, and the belief of the early church about Jesus. Believing in Jesus would have meant believing that the power and presence of God were with him. That power and presence, however, were not primarily manifested in terms of the "divine" qualities of being all powerful and all knowing. Whatever wondrous or miraculous deeds accompanied the preaching of Jesus, together with the charismatic power of that teaching itself, point to something beyond Jesus, namely, the reign of God. Faith in Jesus which is not in touch with what lay at the center of Jesus' own faith runs the risk of elevating Jesus to the status of an idol. It would be tantamount to clinging to Jesus before he had ascended to the Father. Such an attitude toward Jesus is not necessarily dangerous; it does not produce irreparable spiritual harm. But what it does is to privatize Jesus and lead people to want to cling to him in a highly individual relationship. And it also leads to separating Jesus from history and from what happens in our world. The reign of God becomes the kingdom of heaven, not the reconfiguration of this world along the lines of the creator's intention for the human race.

To make Jesus himself into an object of faith effectively empties the gospel story of its real meaning, and this would indeed be unfortunate. Salvation does not come through believing in Jesus, as if the whole business of our religious lives were simply a matter of acknowledging Jesus as our personal Lord and Savior. If believing in Jesus means following his example, then the important thing for us becomes listening to the word of God and putting it into practice. Strictly speaking, salvation is God's transforming us and our world. Salvation is God's refashioning of people and their communities in terms of justice, love and peace. Salvation means our becoming fully mature men and women and liberated from the power of sin and death; it means finally becoming people of compassion. Salvation extends God's creative action into history.

Jesus believed that God's will was to save human beings from *everything* which oppressed them. The power of the gospel story consists in its ability to invite us into Jesus' own faith, and, through that faith, into living and dying for the reign of God. Furthermore, it is not just *any* story about God that can do this. It is the *story of Jesus* which creates the possibility of our hearing and responding to the good news, "The kingdom of God has come near" (Mk 1:15).

With the recovery of the human dimension of Jesus in the gospel story, there also comes a letting go of the divine qualities in terms of which we had been accustomed to think about him. To be sure, the Christ of our faith functions at the practical level like God, but the Jesus of the story speaks and behaves very differently. The people around him accepted him as a teacher and a prophet, a person filled with the Spirit; they would not have approached him as God, nor would Jesus have permitted them to do so. As dramatic as the resurrection is, this event needs to be interpreted carefully. An audience looking for reassurance about the existence of an afterlife is going to "hear" the Easter stories differently from a congregation in need of divine confirmation that God is always on the side of the victims of social and political oppression. A community which could have concluded that the resurrection reveals Jesus' special, even unique relationship with God is on the right track. But it would miss a critical turn if it failed to keep Jesus connected with the reign of God which he had preached and for which he gave his life. Jesus was put to death because of his commitment to the reign of God, not because he had been called to save the human race from its sins.

If Jesus' being raised from the dead does not lead to renewed dedication and struggle on the part of his companions to preaching the reign of God, but instead leads only to a proclamation of Jesus as Savior and God's Son, then followers like Mary Magdalene have their wish and Jesus' return to the Father remains incomplete. We would be viewing Jesus apart from the reign of God which conferred upon his life its context and gave it its fundamental meaning. In short, we would see Jesus without ever knowing the Father.

All of this belongs to the sense of transition within Christian experience today. It might appear that one vector of that transition is from a Christ-centered theology and spirituality to a God-centered spirituality. This reading of things would be partly correct. The Christ-centered spirituality of the past was in fact God-centered, because believers related to him as they would to God. Christ was a sacrament or an icon that mediated the divine mystery for us, although sometimes the fact was forgotten that he was still a sacrament and ought not to be identified with the holy mystery of God purely and simply.

I believe that a more accurate reading of things, however, would be that the direction of the transition has been from a Christ-centered spirituality to a Jesus-centered one. Furthermore, if we follow this trajectory to its likely conclusion, then the movement will continue from a Jesus-centered spirituality to a kingdom-centered one, and with the reign of God assuming central place in our theology and spirituality, Jesus' return to the Father will be complete.

Some in the church have been bothered by the growing emphasis upon the humanness of Jesus. They perceive this as a diminishment of Christian faith and as a loss of the divine element within our religion.

Such a reaction is understandable. The telling of the gospel stories by preachers and teachers often highlighted the miraculous, almost magical details of many scenes and events. Having accepted those versions of the story, a person might feel confused, betrayed, or even downright angry when presented with an account that unlocks the humanity and the everyday world behind the gospels. One person might want simply to walk out of the church altogether. Another might want to condemn and to silence those who are introducing novelties and heresies into the traditional belief. And still another will relish the newer version of the story as liberating and exciting. Each is living through the transition. One wants to swim to shore to escape the force of the current, another attempts to swim against the force, and a third realizes that the currents are not hostile, but friendly.

Terms such as "sin," "the cross," "redemption," "resurrection," "conversion," will refer to different things, depending upon where we anchor them. If we anchor them in the story of Jesus in terms of the reign of God, they will mean one thing. If, however, we situate them in terms of the church's proclamation about Christ as the divine Son of God, then they are going to mean something else. One of the consequences of the recovery of the human, historical Jesus through contemporary biblical scholarship has been a massive redefining of all the categories and doctrines of Christian faith. Resurrection is no longer viewed primarily as proof of the divinity of Jesus, but as confirmation of Jesus' ministry of proclaiming the reign of God and the "proof" that God has taken the side of the oppressed. Divinity is no longer regarded as sharing in the "divine nature," but as being fully human, where being fully human refers to the mature freedom which arises from faithfully attending to the word of God and putting it into practice. Abiding fidelity to the word of God is perhaps the chief mark of being a daughter or son of God, and a brother or sister of Jesus: "Whoever does the will of God is my brother and sister and mother" (Mk 3:35).

"Sin" is not simply a willful violation of the divine law, but the whole range of actions, relationships, attitudes and structures which oppress and dehumanize men and women. The reign of God is not everlasting bliss in heaven, but a reality which has already begun to unfold in this world. It represents a human community consciously living under the Spirit, faithful to the word of God: sharing, forgiving, serving, proclaiming, and seeking and promoting justice.

The cross is not simply the instrument of humanity's ransom from the power of death, but the price Jesus paid for his own commitment to the reign of God and its justice. The cross does not stand alone, as an isolated event within human history, but rather it stands in connection with the whole of Jesus' prophetic ministry.

Redemption is not merely the individual's being forgiven and rescued for eternal life; it is also the divine work of saving people from economic slavery, political oppression and social abandonment. Redemption is also the grace that transforms human communities and societies so that they might be truly humanizing places of shared life and faith.

The first breakthrough, then, takes place when the believer discovers what the story of Jesus was all about. Relating to Jesus through his humanness means understanding what drove him, as it were. It means appreciating the enormously attractive qualities which led the disciples to gather around him as companions, and to dedicate their lives to the reign of God also. The second breakthrough occurs in the realization that above all Jesus was a believer. To be his follower, or his companion, entails sharing his faith and even his experience of God. Our faith rests upon his, both horizontally and vertically. The church's faith in God is its believing in the God of Jesus, who was at the same time the God of Israel: the God of Abraham, Isaac and Jacob; the God of prophets like Elijah, Jeremiah and Amos; the God of women like Esther, Ruth, Hannah and Mary. In other words, we have inherited Jesus' faith.

But our faith not only stretches horizontally or historically back to the prayer and life of Jesus; it also depends, from moment to moment, upon the Spirit of God, which for us has been forever made precise or specific as the Spirit of Jesus. Jesus has been raised from the dead. The force of this claim is its insistence that the work of Jesus continues in and through his brothers and sisters: "We must work the works of him who sent me while it is day" (Jn 9:4). Yet even more importantly, the Spirit of Jesus remains among us as the empowering source of faith, urging us to stay faithful to the story that we have heard, and shaping us into that new creature which God desires us and our communities to be.

3

The Cross in Transition

In his wonderful account of Saint Paul Community Baptist church, *Upon This Rock*, Samuel Freedman tells of a meeting of the "Wounded Healers," a support group of men and women trying to stay clear of drugs and alcohol. The predominantly black congregation of Saint Paul's, located in a New York City neighborhood, is quite familiar with addiction, aimlessness and unemployment; but over the years the revitalized church has brought about a great difference both in the neighborhood and within individual lives. At one of the meetings of the Wounded Healers, a woman speaks:

> "I know Jesus died for me," she stammers through tears. "But I ain't that strong. I'm a human being. I'm weak. I'm not perfect." She drags a tissue across her cheeks, then fingers its texture. "And I know they's excuses."[1]

The woman's statement "I know Jesus died for me" intrigued me. I have heard this sentiment expressed countless times in prayer groups, private conversations and confessions. Through it a person is summoning up the courage to endure some particularly difficult problem or situation. The belief that "Jesus has died for me" contains great motivational power. For if Jesus has given up his life for me, the logic runs, then why am I so slow to reform my own life, or why am I so reluctant to take charge of things and do what I know is right for me? No personal cost or sacrifice will ever be as great as Jesus' sacrifice for me. Knowledge of what Jesus has done uncovers all my pretense: "And I know they's excuses."

Jesus lives for me.

not guilt – hope

"I know Jesus died for me." Through this belief, people have discovered the strength to keep on struggling to overcome temptations. They find the power to continue living, and to grow as human beings. Through this belief, they gradually become liberated from their fears, from their addictions and enslavements, and from their feelings of being worthless. Yet their life, their humanity and their freedom are always related to Jesus, "who died for me," as Saint Paul said: "And the life I now live in the flesh I live by faith in the Son of God, who loved me and gave himself for me" (Gal 2:20).

If we consider the empowering nature of this belief carefully, then it becomes clear that the force of the statement is not so much "Jesus *died* for me" but "Jesus *lives* for me." The fact of the matter is that whatever life is to be experienced through his death only makes sense in view of the fact that Jesus is now alive. It is Jesus' *life* that people discover, a new life which comes to us from the Spirit through Jesus and his story. The strength to remain sober, or to refuse drugs, or to be honest with oneself, or to terminate a bad relationship, or to put the good of others ahead of oneself, or, as the baptismal promise says, "to renounce Satan," is a sign of life. As a result, what keeps the believer steady and willing to keep on trying is not a sense of guilt ("Jesus gave up his life for the sake of this poor, wretched sinner"), but a sense of hope ("Death no longer has any power over Jesus, or over those who believe in his name"). In short, the power within the image of Jesus crucified is the power of the resurrection: "Why do you look for the living among the dead?" (Lk 24:5)

"Jesus lives for me": this is the truly important claim of Christian faith. What this conviction points to is an experience of the gospel story as life-enhancing, and whatever truly enhances life or enables us to surmount our trials can only be of God. The cross turns into a symbol bursting with all sorts of meaning because people find life in it, and the life they discover there is nothing other than the life of God. "Jesus is alive for me" means that Jesus lives and communicates life for our sake. The memory of what he preached and taught, the stories about what he did and what happened to him, continue to challenge men and women many centuries later. They can walk with him, listen to him, watch him and pray with him. Like the first companions of Jesus, they become aware of their limits, they learn to depend upon God, just as Jesus did, and they start to take great risks, like "stepping onto the water" in order to be where Jesus is.

Jesus *lives* for us. The important point is not that Jesus laid down his life for our sake. In fact, such an idea probably does not speak to the experience of many people today, separated by so many centuries from the actual conditions and persons which brought Jesus to his death. There is no conceivable way that any of us can be made responsible for Jesus' death, and there is no convincing way that Jesus' death brought about the forgiveness of sins.[2] First of all, we were not present when Jesus lived and died; and secondly, the God of Israel had always been a God of mercy and compassion, which is why Jesus and his disciples after him could preach repentance. Why repent, unless God is forgiving? It makes a great deal of sense, however, to say that God poured the fullness of life into Jesus for our sake; our being given a share in that new life is the very practical consequence of raising Jesus from the dead. He lives, not for himself, but for us. And the life that he was given through the resurrection is none other than the very life of God, which only the creator can breathe into us.

To some extent, even the cross has been caught up in the transition within our spirituality. Cross and resurrection have always stood together, of course, at least conceptually. But it was hard to escape the tendency to temporalize those moments: first Jesus died, then he was buried, and then he was raised from the tomb. We think death, then we think resurrection. The only meaningful way to hold these moments together, however, is to view them backwards: the resurrection is what interprets the cross and turns it into the great paradox of which Paul wrote:

> For Jews demand signs and Greeks desire wisdom, but we proclaim Christ crucified, a stumbling block to Jews and foolishness to Gentiles, but to those who are called, both Jews and Greeks, Christ the power of God and the wisdom of God. For God's foolishness is wiser than human wisdom, and God's weakness is stronger than human strength (1 Cor 1:22–25).

Or, to cite another of Paul's texts, "power is made perfect in weakness" (2 Cor 12:9). The raising of Jesus is the ultimate sacrament or sign in human history that the power of sin and death has been reversed, for those who love God (Rom 8:28).

It is understandable why older forms of piety placed greater emphasis on the cross than on the resurrection. Because most human lives are marked, at least some time or other, by suffering and diminishment, the sign of the cross corresponded to human experience far more than the resurrection did: the cross transformed human suffering and invested it with a deeper value by associating our suffering with the mystery of Jesus' passion and death. Traditional eucharistic piety, with its stress upon uniting oneself with Jesus' sacrifice and his complete surrender to the will of God, dovetailed with the pain, struggle and tedium which many people experienced. Through the eucharist, they would join themselves to the cross in order that they, too, might be accepted by God and that their suffering might serve some creative purpose.

I think it can be said that the theological perspective of the council tried to restore some balance within Christian piety by focusing more attention on the resurrection. The effort to position the cross and the resurrection together as inseparable parts of the one paschal mystery led some artists, for example, to place the glorified Jesus on the cross. The proclamation of faith which was introduced into the eucharistic liturgy affirms "Christ has died, Christ is risen," because cross and resurrection belong together: one interprets the other. And the revised funeral liturgy clearly took its pitch from Easter faith. It underscored the ultimate fruit of our dying and rising with Christ through baptism.

Yet something else happened, too. The cross used to be presented in terms that fostered individual, private piety: the crucified Jesus was there, hanging on the cross, for me. But as theology concentrated increasingly on the communal dimension of grace and salvation, it was no longer adequate to explain the significance of the cross solely in terms of what Jesus had done for the individual. Jesus was not nailed to me, personally, but to the world. True, the cross tended to turn the spotlight of God's unfathomable love on each one of us; but that love was there even before the cross, and it would have been there regardless of whether or not Jesus had died. Even while we were still sinners, God loved us (Rom 5:8). It is because of God's love for the human race that God undertook the great initiative in choosing Israel to reveal to all the nations what it meant to be people of God, and in calling Jesus to announce that God's reign was finally at hand. What the cross did express was God's solidarity with human beings in their long historical struggle against all the forces which would rob them of their dignity as God's daughters and sons. The cross expressed God's oneness with a world oppressed. When Jesus became one of the victims in that oppression because he protested against the reign of sin and death, his story became in effect a story of God-with-us in the ongoing campaign against injustice, intimidation, fear and despair.

The strength which Christians experience in the cross comes from knowing that God is here with us; when human beings resist evil, or struggle with temptation, or fight for an end to their poverty, they do not resist alone.

Some people will continue to look to the cross as a source of personal strength and inspiration, because the cross gives form to their belief in the love and forgiveness of God. But the love and forgiveness of God can be experienced in other ways apart from the cross. What cannot be separated from the cross, however, is Jesus' oneness with men and women dehumanized by slavery, hunger, persecution, alienation and despair. God's love is revealed in this, of course, because the story of Jesus is telling us that God stands with us even at our worst. Yet there is a potential scandal in the divine choice to join our history. God loves us, but that love is preferential: God has chosen to express the divine solidarity with the human race through taking the side of the poor and oppressed. In a particular way, therefore, it can be said that Jesus died for them. And in an equally special way it can be said that Jesus now lives for them. The life of God that the rest of us draw—the new life of Jesus risen—we shall have to draw through our solidarity with the poor.

4

Transition in the Life of Jesus

The realization that the way things were, or are, is not going to be the way of the future, most likely occurred to Jesus, too. The momentary sense of confusion or disorientation, brought on by an awareness of the limited scope he had of God's saving action in the world, could well have left Jesus realizing at some point in his life that he was caught in a movement that would go beyond anything he could have conceived or envisioned. The gospel provides a number of clues that this might have been the case.

There are several instances in the gospel story where Jesus appears to have been genuinely caught off guard by expressions of faith from the strangest of corners. The Gentiles, at least in many Jewish eyes, were not noteworthy for being believers. One did not ordinarily expect to find faith from them, since "Gentile" referred to the peoples of the world who did not worship the one, true God and who had not been given the law as a route to wisdom and life.

I should point out that any discussion about the relation between Jews and Gentiles calls for some precision. The understanding of Judaism which most of us have originates with the Bible. We are familiar with the Hebrew scriptures (our Old Testament) and the Jews are mentioned frequently in the New Testament writings. Most of the Christians within the first generation would have been Jews who had lived in Palestine. But there were also many Jewish people who lived outside Palestine in the wider non-Jewish world which was greatly influenced by Greek thought and culture, and where Greek was the language of educated people. In that Hellenistic world, Jews occasionally developed an attitude toward non-Jewish thought, values and customs which was more tolerant and receptive than what one would have found in Galilee and Judea. If Jesus had been born and raised in a community of Hellenized Jews, his outlook would obviously have been markedly different from what we see through the refractive light of the gospels. Of course, in that case we would no longer be speaking about Jesus of Nazareth.[3]

Apparently, Jesus viewed his mission in terms of his being sent exclusively to his own people, to the lost sheep of the house of Israel. Only the occasional foreigner who might have converted to the Jewish faith would be included within this mission. While the idea of a devout Gentile, that is, of a "pious non-believer," was not unknown to Jesus and his contemporaries, he might have been truly astonished by the depth of the faith that could issue from such individuals, since, at least by popular definition, the Gentiles were supposed to be godless. One did not expect to find fervent openness to God among the Roman military who occupied the land, or among the Gentile population of the Gerasenes. This attitude might account for Jesus' reaction to the faith of the Canaanite woman and to that of the Roman centurion. In both cases, Jesus expressed surprise and amazement: "Woman, great is your faith!" (Mt 15:28); "Truly I tell you, in no one in Israel have I found such faith" (Mt 8:10).

In each case, the person undertakes to instruct Jesus:

He answered, "I was sent only to the lost sheep of the house of Israel." But she came and knelt before him, saying, "Lord, help me." He answered, "It is not fair to take the children's food and throw it to the dogs." She said, "Yes, Lord, yet even the dogs eat the crumbs that fall from their masters' table" (Mt 15:24–27).

The centurion answered, "Lord, I am not worthy to have you come under my roof; but only speak the word, and my servant will be healed. For I also am a man under authority, with soldiers under me; and I say to one, 'Go,' and he goes, and to another 'Come,' and he comes, and to my slave, 'Do this,' and the slave does it" (Mt 8:8–9).

In the first case, if we take "children's food" to be the word of God as given to those within the household of Israel, then the Canaanite woman has pointed out to Jesus that the same word has to feed "the dogs," that is, the Gentiles who wait at the table of faith. In the second case, the Roman tells Jesus that "waiting on the word" lies at the heart of obedience. Perhaps he wishes to spare Jesus the awkwardness of entering a Gentile home. Perhaps the man is genuinely humble in the presence of such a respected religious figure. In either case, the centurion unwittingly gives Jesus a lesson: the "obedience" of faith is a matter of waiting on the word of God, and he himself is waiting for that word to fall from Jesus' lips. Faith does not depend upon whether or not a person is a descendant of Abraham.

The customary attitude of Palestinian Jews toward the Gentiles adds narrative effect to the tale of the demon-possessed maniac who roamed the tombs of the Gerasene hillside (Mk 5:1–20). Why in the world would Jesus be concerned about the well-being of that nonbeliever, whose closest neighbors were a herd of swine? And why in the world would such a person be commissioned to announce to his Gentile family and friends how much the Lord had done for him? The point seems to be that the capacity to hear the word of God and to spread it is not destroyed even by the presence of innumerable "unclean spirits." In this case, matters are reversed; it is not Jesus who was amazed, but the Gentile people of the Decapolis, who heard the reports of what a Jewish prophet had done for one of the wretched ones among them. And yet, we might ask, could Jesus have failed to be surprised that even such a man as this was capable of experiencing the presence and power of God?

On several occasions, Samaritan figures appear in the gospel story. Their appearance implies that Jesus was challenging his listeners to consider what really made a person an "outsider." Those whom people consider to be unrighteous often turn out to be more righteous or open to God than those who viewed themselves as specially chosen and loved. If God could raise up children to Abraham from the stones of the earth (Lk 3:8), then God could just as surely raise them from among the impoverished, outcast and "godless" peoples of the world. We should beware, in other words, of beholding the world in insider/ outsider terms. At least the Samaritans, unlike the Gentiles, traced their ancestry back to Abraham, and thus could logically be conceived as part of the lost sheep of the house of Israel. But did Jesus always view them this way? It is possible that Jesus would have categorized the

Samaritans, at an early stage of his ministry, as "outsiders." If this was the case, then Jesus, too, had more to learn about the ways of God.

The whole point of the story of the "good" Samaritan turns on a favorable portrayal of a group whom most of Jesus' countrymen would have considered outcasts, and that means that Jesus (following Luke's version of the gospel story) had transcended this prejudice. The one leper who returned to give thanks was not a Jew, but a Samaritan: "Was none of them found to return and give thanks except this foreigner?" (Lk 17:18) Likewise, Jesus recalled for the people of Nazareth the memory that the prophet Elisha had not healed any of the lepers of Israel, but one from godless Syria (Lk 4:27). It is quite likely that what we have here is not so much Jesus' positive attitude toward Samaritans, but Luke's. Nevertheless, it would be hard to conceive of Luke portraying Jesus this way merely to serve Luke's own theological agenda. Furthermore, a major element of the memorable episode in the fourth gospel where Jesus meets a woman of Samaria who had come to draw water from Jacob's well is the point that Jews and Samaritans have no dealings with one another (Jn 4:9). In this scene, it was not Jesus who was amazed, but the disciples (Jn 4:27).

On reviewing these texts, therefore, the reader has to wonder at what point in his life Jesus had developed an attitude toward the Samaritans which was so strikingly different from that of his fellow Jews. It makes little sense to assert that Jesus always thought and behaved this way, as if he never had to learn such things. For to insist that Jesus was beyond having to learn about the ways of God would mean that Jesus never enjoyed the consolation which comes from being surprised by grace. Besides, if Jesus learned something from the Canaanite woman (Mark refers to her as Syrophoenician [7:26]), and if he actually was astonished at the centurion's faith, then it only makes sense to conclude that at some point in his life he learned to see beyond the distinction Jew/Samaritan, insider/outsider, native/foreigner. In fact, everything which Jesus taught he must first have learned in terms of his own experience. Jesus never taught anything in the abstract. He was not like a teacher who merely read from his yellowed notes, passing on to his students in an unthinking fashion the lessons he had been given. There is nothing passive about the gospel; its truths are active, having been churned within the human experience of Jesus.

The truth Jesus was learning, then, was that Israel's God was the
God of the nations before ever becoming the God of Abraham. And no
matter how much his religious tradition, the tradition of the people of
Israel, reinforced both their sense of election and their sense that the
true God belonged to them, the fact remained that God had never
changed. The fact that God had showed himself to Israel, and revealed
to them the divine name, did not mean that God had done nothing
like this for any other nation. And the fact that God was so concerned
about the Jewish slaves in Egypt did not mean that God was not equally
concerned about slavery and oppression in the rest of the world. Jesus'
experience appears to have been pointing him in the direction of a
profound, if not altogether clear revelation. God was as concerned
about the Romans, the neighboring Gentile population that lived
across Israel's borders, the villages of Samaria, and the Greeks (Jn 7:35,
12:20), as God was about the people of Israel.

We may never know how this insight gradually wove itself into the
way Jesus thought of himself, his mission and his conception of the
reign of God. We are left with only an occasional glimpse into the
universal orientation of his faith: "Then people will come from east
and west, from north and south, and will eat in the kingdom of God"
(Lk 13:29). And again: "I tell you, many will come from east and west
and will eat with Abraham and Isaac and Jacob in the kingdom of
heaven" (Mt 8:11). Ultimately, the role of the Gentiles in God's plan
was something Jesus had to leave in God's hands. Jesus himself would
not directly be the agent or messenger who would bring God's word to
the nations. He could be no more than someone who would illumi-
nate the way ("a light of revelation to the Gentiles" [Lk 2:32]). Nevertheless, the reign of God would one day belong to them, too.

Jesus' attitude toward the Temple may reveal a further element in
his sense of transition. No doubt, in the beginning, the Temple played
a major role in Jesus' religious awareness. It was, after all, the center of
Israel's life and worship. Luke, of course, locates Jesus in the Temple at
an early age, where he is pictured as conversing with the teachers, and
Jesus is remembered as referring to the Temple as "my Father's house"
(Lk 2:49; Jn 2:16). John places the episode of the cleansing of the
Temple at the beginning of Jesus' public ministry, which suggests that
Jesus envisioned himself as sent to cleanse and purify the Temple, or

rather, what the Temple represented. The cleansing of the Temple, in other words, would have anticipated the cleansing of the people through repentance and renewed faith.

Yet by the end of his public ministry, Jesus' appearance in the Temple suggests the passing of this particular institution. Its barrenness or lack of fruit points to its future destruction. But if the Temple was doomed to fade because it was incapable of responding to the word of Jesus and renewing itself, then clearly Jesus would have experienced this as a sense of loss. Otherwise, it would be hard to explain why Jesus would "weep" over Jerusalem:

> As he came near and saw the city, he wept over it, saying, "If you, even you, had only recognized on this day the things that are for your peace! But now they are hidden from your eyes" (Lk 19:41).

Jesus wept, because he cared about his people and their religious institutions. If he had not cared about them, he would never have taken his mission to the holy city of his ancestors.

Needless to say, we can do little more than conjecture how Jesus responded to the transition which was taking place around him. The prophets had come and gone, although their words and example still hung in the air. So, too, John the Baptist: he was called, he preached, and he was executed. But again, the sureness and intensity of John's voice could not be so easily silenced. To live in Israel was to breathe John's hope. Jesus might well have realized that he, too, would pass, as would the heavens and the earth. The word of God, however, would remain forever, the only fixed point in the great temporal currents of revolution, change, and transition. Jesus might have reacted to the events of his time purely and simply in terms of a faith which reached out to embrace an unknown future: "Yet, not my will but yours be done" (Lk 22:42) and "Father, into your hands I commend my spirit" (Lk 23:46). Each of these sayings reflects the way faith creates a means of passage when everything else seems confused, uncertain or even lying in ruins.

5

The Cross: What Happened at the End?

For many of us, the cross of Jesus represents the focal point of the gospel story. Christmas is warm and endearing, and Easter is joyful; but the cross is what strikes us as most real and serious. By the time we reach adulthood, life has showed us its hard side. The symbol of the cross helps us to interpret and deal with rejection, suffering, struggle, defeat and humiliation. The cross pulls human suffering into the suffering of Jesus, endowing it with a higher meaning and value, and it enables men and women to endure patiently, even sometimes gladly, the burdensome side of being human. After all, would we not prefer affective and spiritual wholeness, whatever the cost, than to remain stuck in the emotional world of our childhood or adolescence? Would we not choose wisdom and liberty of soul, whatever the inner struggle and sacrifice, than to be paralyzed by timidity, or the lack of self-knowledge, or guilt? Would we not rather pick up our "cross" daily and follow Jesus into being fully a son or daughter of God, than lose our humanity to the power of sin? As a symbol, the cross "succeeds" by connecting the mystery of God with human suffering. Whoever lives under the sign of the cross, therefore, is going to experience the presence of God in the most unlikely of places, since one does not ordinarily associate God with diminishment, pain, injustice and death. On the contrary, God is usually associated with victory, power, freedom, justice and life.

The experience of God in the darkest moments of human life is hard to put into words. Hence, the need for a symbol or sign that can transform such moments by investing them with a higher sort of logic, which is intelligible through faith: God can be present even when one feels the divine absence. The cry, "My God, my God, why have you forsaken me?" (Mk 15:34), led at least one bystander to reach a surprising conclusion:

> Now when the centurion, who stood facing him, saw that in this way he breathed his last, he said, "Truly this man was God's Son!" (Mk 15:39)

Why should a cry of abandonment elicit such a reaction from Gentile lips? Clearly, the evangelist saw no contradiction here; absence and presence, God and not-God are joined, almost naturally.

Whether or not Jesus actually said those words attributed to him on the cross is something we shall never be absolutely certain about. One could imagine an early Christian storyteller, who was familiar with Psalm 22, placing those words on Jesus' lips; they comprise the opening line of a special type of prayer. If so, then perhaps the storyteller at that point of the narrative would interrupt his recounting of the passion of Jesus to recite the entire psalm. If Jesus himself actually spoke those words from the cross, then obviously Jesus was praying that psalm in a manner he had never prayed it before. In either case, what we have is an instance of prayer at the moment of darkness. Although Jesus might not have had the strength to recall or speak them, the other verses of Psalm 22 breathe confidence and courage. The words of abandonment, therefore, stand out, not because they are untypical of Jesus' experience of God, but because to whom else would he cry at that very moment, except to God?

> Yet it was you who took me from the womb;
>   you kept me safe on my mother's breast.
> On you was I cast from my birth,
>   and since my mother bore me you have been my God (Psalm 22:9–10).

The piety or devotion with which we are accustomed to approach the cross needs to be set aside for a moment, if we are fully to appreciate the prayer of Jesus. Jesus on the cross was not pondering sophisticated theological notions like redemption, eternal salvation, sacrificial atonement, or the forgiveness of sins. These are the major categories the church later employed to interpret the cross and probe its mystery. Even the meditative recourse to Psalm 22 on the part of our early storyteller represents an effort to reconcile the scandal of the cross with the well-known faith of Jesus: in other words, to make sense of a horrible, tragic event. The prophet who trusted in the word of God like no one else found himself utterly forsaken by the God he served.

But if we set these efforts aside, then what we have to deal with is Jesus' own experience of disorientation and failed expectation. Where was God now? What had happened to the reign of God? How could a mission which had begun so joyously and enthusiastically wind up totally disarrayed? Had God actually been there, in the beginning, at the Jordan River and in those ensuing days in the wilderness? Or was that sense of being specially called and loved merely an illusion? Does God use susceptible human beings to further some obscure divine plan, and then drop them in the ash heap of history? Can God be trusted? Or does God simply inspire people with a vision of how things might be, only to leave them stranded when that vision fails to materialize?

The cross, then, brings us face-to-face with some of the hardest elements of the human experience of God. For us, it is also a paradigm of the moment of transition. Jesus had believed wholeheartedly that God was about to inaugurate something new for the people of Israel. What he referred to as the reign of God involved far more than personal interior renewal and private moral reform. The reign of God would have far-reaching effects even within the political, social and economic spheres. Gradually, Jesus may have caught sight more sharply of the universality of Israel's God and realized that God's saving, liberating love extended to all the peoples of the world. Perhaps a humble, "pagan" woman on her knees had opened his eyes to this.

But the reign of God failed to arrive, and by the eve of Jesus' death, prospects of its coming could never have looked bleaker. There had been no final, victorious divine sign confirming Jesus' teaching and establishing the reign of God. The mighty ones still sat securely on their thrones, the poor remained as destitute as ever, the prisoners still languished in dungeon chains, and the good news seemed to have fallen on the most barren of soil. Easter did not change any of this, either, for whatever the resurrection meant, it did not mean that the reign of God, as Jesus envisioned and proclaimed it, had suddenly dawned.

We have to conclude, then, that with his crucifixion Jesus passed into the eternal night, not knowing what would happen next, unsure of God's power to make good on the divine promise, and probably wondering whether he had been misled by the message and spirit of John the Baptist. The mission of Jesus had entered its time of transition. In a way that certainly went beyond what Jesus could have seen at that moment, the God of Israel was indeed about to become the God of the nations. And this was about to take place as a result of the faith of Jesus: his own faith in the God of his ancestors and the divine promise given to them, and his own prophetic witness to the imminent arrival of God's reign.

6

Was Jesus a Contemplative?

The terms "action" and "contemplation" have enjoyed a prominent place in Christian spirituality. Like the terms "faith" and "practice," they point to the necessary balance which must regulate Christian life. It is not enough merely to confess with one's lips that Jesus is Lord; one must also do the will of God (Mt 7:21). It is not enough just to listen to the word of God; one must also keep it, by putting it into practice (Lk 8:21). Faith alone, without works, is dead (Jas 2:26). Since "works" is another way of talking about how fully we love one another, then clearly a person who does not love has never known God, no matter how much he or she professes to be a believer: "Whoever does not love does not know God, for God is love" (1 Jn 4:8).

Action and contemplation, therefore, are often correlative to faith and practice. The action which the word of God demands of us is impossible unless the person is centered in God. Immersion in action, no matter how good and beneficial the activity, which does not proceed from a soul centered in God, can easily lead to a hardness of heart. Meditation and prayer, no matter how intense and consoling, which do not lead to a mindfulness of the world, will eventually prove fatal to the life of the gospel. Even in the case of those whom the Spirit invites to the deepest of interior lives—those who choose to live apart in monastic communities, the chronically ill and infirm, the elderly who have lost their youthful energy and mobility—prayer itself, insofar as it is Christian, increasingly encompasses the whole of humanity. What one formerly might have expressed through action and works now one expresses through love and compassion.

The impulse to identify oneself through feeling and concern with the whole human race is a mark of the Spirit and an organic develop-

MYSTICISM OF THE CROSS

ment of Christian prayerfulness. One learns to embrace the groaning
world, as Jesus did (and Paul after him), by being "nailed" to it. Such
people carry the world in their hearts, feeling its burden, comprehend-
ing its sinfulness, sharing its anxieties and its hopes, and loving it
unreservedly. This is the mysticism of the cross, and it is beautifully
expressed in the celebrated opening paragraph of the council's Pastoral
Constitution on the Church in the Modern World:

> The joys and hopes and the sorrows and anxieties of people today,
> especially of those who are poor and afflicted, are also the joys and
> hopes, sorrows and anxieties of the disciples of Christ, and there is
> nothing truly human which does not also affect them. Their com-
> munity is composed of people united in Christ who are directed by
> the holy Spirit in their pilgrimage towards the Father's kingdom
> and who have received the message of salvation to be communi-
> cated to everyone. For this reason it feels itself closely linked to the
> human race and its history.[4]

compassion

The answer to the question, "Was Jesus a contemplative?" requires that we understand what being a contemplative means. In light
of what we just said, surely Jesus was. The gospel recalls the reaction of
Jesus when he realized how much people thirsted for the word of God,
and to what lengths they would go to be able to hear it:

> Now many saw them going and recognized them, for they hurried
> there on foot from all the towns and arrived ahead of them. As he
> went ashore, he saw a great crowd; and he had compassion for
> them, because they were like sheep without a shepherd (Mk 6:33–
> 34).

The compassion Jesus felt toward this crowd was characteristic of his
attitude toward all of his people, and indeed, toward all men and
women. Compassion is the principal mark of a heart and mind which
are authentically contemplative, since compassion is how God sees the
world; to see and feel the world with "tender mercy," as God does (Lk
1:78), is to behold all things with transformed vision. This attitude
sheds light on the reaction of the Samaritan in one of Jesus' stories,
where the unlikely savior came near to the wretched victim, "and when

he saw him, he was moved with pity" (Lk 10:33). The capacity or the readiness to be "moved with pity" under circumstances like these, that is, in a "seeing" which transcends distinctions like Samaritan/Jew and perceives there instead one's sister or brother, is what makes human eyes contemplative.[5]

The word "contemplation" derives from the Latin word for temple (*templum*). The *templum* referred to a place designated by a seer where certain rituals would be performed. Initially, "to contemplate" referred to standing in a place where one could take in with a single glance every direction, in other words, to be in a place with an unobstructed view of the heavens and the earth. But the initial meaning can be extended. To view all things with eyes unobstructed by prejudice or hatred, or to state the point positively, to behold all things with tenderness and love is an accurate way to describe the divine perspective: the divine eye grasps the entire expanse of heaven and earth, past and present, with a single glance. Finding the sacred spot from which we, too, can see the whole world clearly and with love is another way of describing the work of contemplation.[6]

A description of contemplation in terms of compassion is important if we are to distinguish what Jesus was from what he was not. Jesus was not a recluse or a renowned ascetic. Indeed, he would not have fit into our picture of an institutional religious person. He did not belong to a religious community, and he never pronounced religious vows of poverty, chastity and obedience. Jesus did not withdraw from the world in order to protect himself from its distractions and allurements, and thereby to possess the peace and solitude from which to formulate great ideas about the mystery of God. Jesus drew on ordinary life for the images and metaphors he needed to express himself. He did so because he lived and thought in an ordinary, everyday world, where people might run out of food just when an unexpected guest arrives (Lk 11:5–6), or where people have to patch their clothes (Mk 2:21), or where a son might run away and squander his youth (Lk 15:11ff.), or where women sweep their homes (Lk 15:8), or where an accountant is discovered to be crooked (Lk 16:1–8), or where a young child can be suddenly struck by a fatal illness (Mk 5:22–23). The list would be virtually endless. Yet what all these allusions point to is Jesus' being really at home in the everyday world of his people. He thought and imagined in these terms, because this was the only world he knew.

If Jesus was neither a monk nor an ascetic, neither was he a cleric nor a professional theologian. While most people would probably register little surprise over this, I believe the point is worth underlining. My own outlook on Jesus was formed through a long period of Catholic education, mainly at the dedicated hands of religious women and priests. Not only was it a priest who usually spoke about Jesus and preached on the gospels, but the ones who handed on the story of Jesus through religion classes and catechism were religious professionals. The priest was presented to us as "another Christ," whose place he took at the celebration of the mass or in the hearing of confessions.

By the time I was ordained, the neatness of this priestly identity had started to unravel; and within ten years it had come apart completely. As much as I wanted to think of myself as like Jesus, Jesus was not like me in my role as a priest, or in my affiliation with a religious community, or in my professional work as someone trained in theology. The problem, however, was not that my view of Jesus had come apart (actually, it had, and that was troublesome enough). The real problem was that, unconsciously, these identifications or associations had also influenced that way I heard and thus retold the gospel story. They had conditioned the image of Jesus which I preached and taught. At the risk of oversimplifying things which were probably more complex than I shall ever appreciate, the alternative was either to form my picture of Jesus in terms of the institution which I officially represented, or to find a means of letting the gospel story of Jesus refashion my view of the institution and what it meant to be a priest.

To insist that Jesus was not a priest is to place those of us who are ordained on guard, lest we unconsciously separate Jesus from his people. We will do this, if we believe, in our heart of hearts, that Jesus was actually more like us in the way that we have come to define and live out our priestly identity. Furthermore, the people will allow us to get away with this because, while they may not be fully aware of it, the Jesus to whom they have been introduced is less like them than he is like the professional religious people. The qualities stressed, the purpose of his life, the calling of apostles upon which to found a church, the sacrificial nature of his death, all support a view of Jesus in keeping with his being different, apart, sacerdotal and even hierarchical. Jesus was "above" his apostles as some ordained ministers are "above" others, and all the ordained are "above" ordinary people. While this idea itself has certainly been deconstructed in the years since Vatican II, its force lingers in the way the story of Jesus is told and handed on.

There are other profiles which do not fit Jesus, either.[7] He was not a social reformer, nor was he, strictly speaking, the founder of a new religion. Clearly, the message of Jesus called for reform, and a major area of reform was society, including its economic and political institutions. But for Jesus reform never meant the pursuit of equal opportunity and political fairness, it never meant the redistribution of land and goods, or the wholesale resistance to injustice and oppression— activities which might define the work of a social reformer—apart from an all-encompassing and pervasive faith in the God of Israel. It was his conviction that God was concerned about the desperately poor, those surviving at the edge of society, and those deprived of justice, that brought Jesus into conflict with the political and religious establishments of his day. What Jesus saw around him could never be divorced from his own experience of God, Israel's memories about what God had done in the past, the instruction and attitudes imparted to him by Mary and Joseph (a "righteous" man), the powerful witness of John the Baptist, and God's promise always to walk with the children of Abraham. The only category that readily applied to Jesus would be that of the prophet: "a prophet mighty in deed and word before God and all the people" (Lk 24:19).

To say that Jesus was not the founder of a world religion takes some getting used to; it also calls for a qualification. Jesus' intention was to reform the house of Israel, to seek out and to save what was lost: Israel's people, its leaders and its institutions. Although he gathered a group around him, it would be going too far to say that through this Jesus was envisioning the church as we have come to know it. The community around Jesus, especially when it took meals together, became a sign of the reign of God. People wanted to be where Jesus was. They wanted to hear him, they wanted to speak with him, they treasured his companionship: in short, they loved him. He never declined a luncheon or dinner invitation, so far as we know. He never refused to drink, for fear of giving scandal or for fear that some of his companions might imbibe excessively. And he never excluded anyone from table fellowship. In fact, all were welcome at the table where Jesus ate. The fact that rich and poor, sinner and righteous, the powerful and the disenfranchised, the clean and the unclean could recline together at table, in the company of Jesus, was itself a preeminent indication that the reign of God had arrived.

The events which took place after the death of Jesus were no longer in his hands. God, we might say, had designs on the life of Jesus which went beyond anything Jesus could have foreseen (the same thing holds true for each of us). Jesus' movement led to the establishment of communities of those who followed him. At first, they saw no contradiction between being simultaneously Jewish and "Christian." As time passed, however, conflicts and tensions arose which forced a definitive separation of the two groups. Naturally, Christians would look back at the gospel story and watch Jesus in the process of establishing a new dispensation, a new covenant, and a new religion. They might account for the break with Judaism in terms of Jesus' being rejected by his own people; their rejection provided the warrant for the offer of salvation being extended to the Gentiles.

Nevertheless, what slowly evolved into a new religion cannot claim Jesus as its founder without qualification. It was men and women continuing to believe and act in the Spirit of Jesus who "founded" the church, and the church remains faithful to its foundation in the Spirit insofar as it remains faithful to the story of Jesus. Between Jesus and the church there has to be a continuity of aims. For Jesus, it was the reign of God. For the church, it must be the same: praying and working that God's will for the world be done ("Your kingdom come" [Lk 11:2]). On the part of the church, this demands vigilance, lest it substitute its own institutional interests for the primary concern of Jesus' life. One thinks, for example, of how the church has invoked the fact that Jesus was male to defend its practice of ordaining only men. Or again, how the tradition has distilled features of Jesus' life to create the ideal pattern of religious observance in terms of poverty and obedience. Or how it has highlighted the fact that Jesus was single to promote celibacy among its clergy and religious. But at the same time the church appears to have ignored the abiding import of Jesus' Jewish faith in the ongoing process of its self-understanding. This is something that merits further reflection.

7

The Church: What Happened after Jesus?

At the end of his study into the early divorce that took place between Judaism and Christianity, James Dunn observed:

> *Christianity began as a movement of renewal breaking through the boundaries first within and then round the Judaism of the first century.* At its historic heart Christianity is a protest against any and every attempt to claim that God is our God and not yours, God of our way of life and not yours, God of "our" civilization and not yours. Against any and every tendency to designate others as "sinners," as beyond the pale of God's saving grace, or to insist that for sinners to receive forgiveness they must become righteous, that is "righteous" as *we* count "righteousness." Against any and every attempt to mark off some of God's people as more holy than others, as exclusive channels of divine grace over against others. At its heart it is a protest against every attempt to pigeon hole and institutionalize the grace of God, to limit that grace in its expression to the safe confines that human minds can cope with and human capacities can organize. At its heart is an openness to the unexpectedness of divine grace, to the new thing which God may wish to do, even when it breaks through and leaves behind the familiar paths and forms. At its heart is the conviction that God revealed himself most fully not just in human word but in human person, not just in rational or even inspired propositions but in the human relationships which can never be confined within words and formulae alone.[8]

Dunn examined four "pillars" of the Judaism of Jesus' day—the Temple, the covenant and law, election or chosenness, and belief in the oneness of God (monotheism)—and showed how, with respect to each of these, Jesus' attitude would still have left him within the Jewish mainstream. While Jesus expressed outrage at some of the transactions taking place under the Temple's umbrella, he did not want to unmake it altogether, as his enemies alleged.

Similarly, while Jesus' message implied a critique of the way the law and Israel's sense of election had excluded people on the basis of a false view of righteousness, Jesus never intended to undo either the law or the covenant, nor did he intend to discard Israel's sense of having been especially chosen and loved by God. Finally, Jesus certainly subscribed to Israel's traditional confession about the oneness of God, which he, like everyone else, would have proclaimed daily in the great *Shema* prayer: "Hear, O Israel: The Lord is our God, the Lord alone. You shall love the Lord your God with all your heart, and with all your soul, and with all your might" (Deut 6:4–5). It can be said, then, that "For all the ferment he caused, this Jesus could have been absorbed and retained within a Judaism which did not become Christianity."[9]

If Jesus is thus situated firmly within the Judaism of his day, what happened that stretched the ties between the early Christian communities and their Jewish matrix to the point of breaking? Dunn explains that it was along the lines of these four pillars that the cracks began to appear. The Christian communities for various reasons slowly broke away from the Temple and what it had represented in Jewish faith. They broke away from the Torah and from Israel's sense of exclusiveness, which was so much a part of its understanding of the covenant and its sense of being chosen. Finally, they began to make claims about Jesus that devout Jews could not in conscience assent to because those claims would have violated their sense of the oneness of God. The curious result was that while Jesus' disciples of several generations later conveniently embraced the new expression of faith which had emerged, Jesus himself would have been completely out of place there.

Whereas Jesus had initiated a reform movement within Judaism, his followers turned that movement into a new religion, the focus of which was Jesus rather than the kingdom of God which Jesus had proclaimed. Jesus saw himself as God's messenger: what was to be contemplated was the message, not the one who announced it. In his own person, Jesus came to be viewed as the bearer of salvation, so that people would be "saved" through faith in him. Salvation conceived as God's liberating love within this world, transforming or redeeming the present reality and all the structures which make and define us, had slipped from view. Instead, salvation was portrayed as God's gracious gift to those who put their trust in the name of Jesus. The social, historical and horizontal dimension of salvation which figured so prominently into the notion of the reign of God had been replaced by an act of faith in the Son of God.

Would Jesus' sense of his mission have changed, if he had lived longer? While it is impossible to answer this, one could probably guess that, given the apocalyptic expectations of his day, Jesus could never have escaped the overriding conviction that "God has acted and is acting in history to fulfill the promises of Scripture and to inaugurate the new age."[10] Yet neither would it be unthinkable that Jesus might have eventually "burned out," had he lived another fifteen or twenty years. Could the same intense activity have continued indefinitely without some sign from heaven confirming his ministry? Would his ministry have taken an inward turn, so that in his old age Jesus might have become a spiritual master whom people would consult for sage advice, directions on how to meditate, or for encouragement? Would the prophetic denunciations of abuse have given way to composing pious tracts meant to arouse people from their sinful ways?

And how might such a Jesus have renewed himself? Where would he have gone to nourish his own soul and deepen his faith? Where might his inspiration have come from, given the failure of God's reign to materialize?

Again, the only recourse Jesus would have had was to ponder further Israel's great texts and to meditate on the divine promise. There, in the story of his people, Jesus would have repeatedly encountered the overriding conviction of Israel that God moves actively within history to fashion a people and to form a world ever more just. In short, Jesus had allowed himself to be pulled into God's involvement with the world; the God Jesus knew did not reside on mountain tops, or within monastery walls out in the desert, or even upon the temple mount in the holy city. Jesus' religious spirit was shaped by the people and tradition of which he was an integral part. If, as Christians, we firmly believe that "God revealed himself most fully not just in human word but in human person," then the particular shape and orientation of Jesus' religious experience becomes normative for us. Jesus cannot be detached from his Jewish background without distorting the way he reveals God to us.

Does this mean, then, that Christianity has somehow failed Jesus? Does this mean that the church, which believes itself guided by the Spirit, has for many centuries been unfaithful to the story of Jesus? Let us address these issues one by one.

First, the church's belief that it has been guided by the Spirit (and consequently protected against error) needs to be examined closely. The fact is that the church—the individuals who belong to it as well as the institution itself—has not been sinless throughout its history. Over the ages, the church has been rocked by the severest of scandals; even the most cursory reading of its history will spot the gross contradictions between what the church proclaims and what it often practices. Even the idea that the development of its doctrine, the emergence of the "truths" of faith, has always been immune both from individual human arrogance and hatred as well as from ideologies of greed and "power politics," is unconvincing. Even today, the institutional church is slow to admit its mistakes; admitting them several centuries after the fact provides no consolation to the ones initially offended.

Perhaps the clearest examples of the church's being guided by the Spirit are the occasional prophetic outbursts throughout history which have criticized the church's failure to live according to the gospel. The Spirit's abiding concern for the church is more evident in the witnesses to truth who have called attention to the church's compromising, its timidity, its fear of anything new or "modern," its defensiveness, or its abuse of persons and groups, than in its ability to stay the institutional course charted by its leaders. One recalls St. Paul's expectation that there would be prophets within the Christian communities, for the presence of prophets signifies that those communities are alive, that there is healthy tension within them as they struggle to remain faithful to the gospel. A community without prophets is a community gone flat, even dead: the Spirit is no longer there to awaken it from its torpor, or to free it from rigidity by warming frozen hearts and minds.[11]

Second, Jesus cannot be separated from the reign of God without rendering him radically un-Jewish, or at least radically unhistorical. The reign of God was the center of his life and teaching; he lived and died for it. To allow Jesus, rather than the reign of God, to become the object of faith distorts the meaning of discipleship. True, the reign of God did not arrive in the way Jesus had hoped and envisioned. But while the reign of God cannot be divorced from Jesus, it certainly can be detached from the apocalyptic worldview within first-century Palestine. The fact that the kingdom did not come in power, as Jesus had hoped, did not mean that there was no kingdom, or that the kingdom was really not of this world but of the next one. The task of proclaiming the word of God and announcing the good news about God's reign had to continue, if the world itself—the whole human race—was to be liberated from oppression.

I suspect that the early failure to keep the mission of Jesus alive in its fullness, or the early tendency to spiritualize the life and teaching of Jesus and to concentrate salvation in terms of the forgiveness of sins and life in the world to come, occurred because the non-Jewish Christians did not share Israel's hope in the divine promise for liberation by a Messiah in this world. The "Messiah" had come and, for those who had eyes to realize it, this crucified Messiah had in fact liberated the human race from the bondage of sin. Suppose, however, that the early communities had concluded that they would be most faithful to the memory of Jesus by becoming "messianic communities." Suppose they had determined to continue doing what Jesus had done with and among the poor, challenging the mighty ones and championing the cause of the oppressed? If they had viewed themselves as inheriting Jesus' messianic side, then hope in the reign of God would have been the great Christian legacy to all ages as a possibility in this world. The reign of God would have been framed, not in apocalyptic terms, but in terms of humanity's ongoing struggle for justice and freedom. In fact, of course, that struggle has persisted, because men and women have been persistently locked in poverty and injustice throughout history. But the mission to free them by overcoming the structures which kept them oppressed and dehumanized was not the mission which defined the church's understanding of human salvation. It became somewhat secondary, and at times it was even forgotten.

When the church left its Jewish matrix and spread roots into the Greco-Roman world, it lost touch with the historical experience of Israel. The price the church paid for this passage, however, was very high, because the historical experience of Israel was paradigmatic of the experience of oppressed peoples everywhere. And losing touch with that experience, it also lost touch with the overriding concerns of Israel's God, who was and who remains for all time the God of Jesus.

Third, something did happen through the life and death of Jesus of enormous importance. As a result of Jesus' life, there was a new story about God to be told. And in raising Jesus from the dead, God worked the great reversal: the God of Israel was indeed the God of the nations. The God who had been God-for-Israel was now revealed as God-for-all-people. What God had promised Israel was now being offered to all the nations. Through the resurrection it became clear that what God was ready to do for Israel in its oppression, God was likewise ready to do for all his daughters and sons of every time and place. Israel's story was thus to be humanity's "classic" story about God.[12]   *David Tracy*

Finally, most of those who study the New Testament today acknowledge the variety of perspectives embodied there. On the basis of the New Testament itself, one can conceive various expressions of Christian belief about Jesus which would be considered orthodox. The faith of the very first generation of disciples included belief in Jesus as the risen Lord, but this belief did not logically lead them to reject their Jewish roots, or their going to the Temple to worship, or their daily recitation of Israel's traditional prayers. After all, Paul himself on occasion returned to the Temple to pray to the God of his ancestors and make an offering. While their belief about Jesus risen would certainly have reconfigured the way they thought about the God of Israel, Jesus' resurrection was not the only thing the disciples believed in.

Yet the New Testament also contains expressions of belief about Jesus which would have made devout Jewish Christians uncomfortable. While they would have had no difficulty accepting Jesus as "risen Lord" and acknowledging him as Israel's Messiah, they could not have accepted him as the Son of God in a sense which would have compromised their belief in the oneness of God. Most of us find no difficulty with this confession; in our understanding of Christian faith Jesus is frequently identified with God. We pray to Jesus as we would to God.

We need to ask ourselves, however, whether we mean to pray to Jesus and to God as if to two individuals. If so, then something is clearly wrong, because God is not an individual. The person and image of Jesus mediates for us the presence of God; we find God in Jesus. Yet to identify God and Jesus purely and simply, without any qualification whatsoever, is extremely misleading. For one thing, this would overlook entirely the fact that Jesus himself addressed God in prayer as Father. Jesus provides the "way" to the Father, but he is not the Father; and it is to the Father that all prayer is ultimately directed.

The challenge posed to Christian faith in this time of transition is that it should recover its Jewish roots and own them. This marks a unique moment in the church's life. For perhaps the first time since its origins, the church is in a position to view itself clearly in terms of the faith tradition from whence it came. Centuries of prejudice have been uncovered or portrayed for what they were. The anti-Semitism of the past appears all the more horrendous: for not only was it disgusting and evil in human terms as an abuse of people made in God's image, as all of us are; it was also faithless to the memory of Jesus.

Needless to say, we have to be careful not to level all the differences between these two religions, which are clearly continuous at many points. Hans Küng warns us that "the opposition between Jews and Christians [cannot be] reduced to one long, two-thousand-year-old misunderstanding."[13] I would suggest that the theological root of their continuity lies in the fact that the God who creates and who formed the people of Israel is the same God who raised Jesus from the dead and called forth the church. The root of their discontinuity lies in the fact that the God of Israel has broken through ethnic and cultural boundaries to become the God of the nations, and in the fact that the story of Jesus, for Christians, has become normative for understanding God's relationship to the human race. By this I do not mean to suggest that there had been no scriptural voices sounding a universal note. The gospel narrative draws upon an important text from Isaiah, which may be worth recalling:

And the foreigners who join themselves to the Lord, to minister to him, to love the name of the Lord, and to be his servants, all who keep the sabbath, and do not profane it, and hold fast my covenant—these I will bring to my holy mountain, and make them joyful in my house of prayer; their burnt offerings and their sacrifices will be accepted on my altar; for my house shall be called a house of prayer for all peoples (Isa 56:6–7; see Mk 11:17).

Yet the universal vision of Isaiah beholds the nations coming to Jerusalem, and this indeed represents a theological breakthrough; but the point I am making is that the identity of Israel's God did not depend upon an identification with Jerusalem. Which is why Stephen could declare that "the Most High does not dwell in houses made with human hands" (Acts 7:48), and why Jesus could say to the woman at the well, "Woman, believe me, the hour is coming when you will worship the Father neither on this mountain nor in Jerusalem" (Jn 4:21).

One of my theology professors used to punctuate the prayer that ended his lectures with "Thanks be to God and his Jewish mother." We smiled, naturally, each time. But behind this lay a profound insight which the tradition would have done well to dwell on: in Christian imagination, and according to the Christian story, everything begins with Israel's God, revealed as Emmanuel, God-with-us. This being-with-us of God is another way of starting to think about the reign of God. And it is our faith and hope in the reign of God which must be recovered. For this, we need to sink the roots of our souls within the soil of Israel's historical experience.

Thanks be to God
and His Jewish mother.

PART THREE
GETTING OUR BEARINGS
IN A TIME OF TRANSITION

1

Is God's Business Always Religious?

A former Archbishop of Canterbury once cautioned: "It is a mistake to suppose that God is only, or even chiefly, concerned with religion."[1] The fact of the matter is that while religion concerns itself with the things of God, the divine interest in our regard extends to the whole of human life. God's creative intention is that we should become fully human, fully alive as God's daughters and sons. But this intention cannot be fulfilled apart from the redemption and humanization of all the groups, institutions, values and ways of thinking which figure into the way we live and mature. Our becoming fully human is not an individual affair between each human being and God, as if the only thing that truly mattered was our personal moral or spiritual well-being, the very thing which is commonly considered to be religion's proper sphere. The full creation of the human being does not occur outside of our involvement in communities and societies. What sort of human being we become is going to be conditioned by what happens in our homes and families, by the political and financial structures and values of the country in which we have to live and work, by the values and assumptions of our culture and the social class to which we belong. A man or a woman brought up in a home where people scream at and abuse one another, or where promises cannot be trusted, is going to be in a very different position from someone raised in a home where the parents remained faithful and caring. Someone raised on the brink of poverty is going to look at life differently from someone nurtured on privilege and opportunity. Indeed, we have even seen the paradoxical emergence of a new class of inner-city heroes. In neighborhoods steeped in the drug subculture young men returning from prison are often regarded as role models unwittingly forged by the system that imprisoned them.

For good or ill, we are formed (or deformed) by the ideals, expectations and attitudes of the communities to which we belong. The only way to see "through" our experience, whether in our family life, our work, the political and financial arrangements that dictate how we relate to one another, the circles of our social life, or even in the church, is through the process which the gospel calls conversion. On the personal level this usually means change of heart, an awareness of the desires, actions and habits that have crippled our ability to think and act clearly and truthfully, accompanied by an awareness of how limited is our outlook on people, the world and life itself. Sometimes we call such limitation "sin." My favorite gospel story about this inversion of perspective is Peter's outburst that he was a sinful man when Jesus, with no experience of fishing and no familiarity with the waters of the lake, instructed Peter and his companions where to cast their nets (Lk 5:1–11). Peter's sinfulness did not refer, at that moment, to some particular act or omission; it seemed to consist of his reluctance to open his mind and heart beyond the confines of the world and routine he knew so well. The sheer familiarity of his world could block God's effort to intrude and to change things by its utter predictability.

But conversion can also occur at the level of community life, too. Communities can break through their habitual way of relating to one another, or the way they see and categorize the stranger, the one who does not belong to the group. Communities can become mindful of their limited worldview and their sinfulness, the way they have blocked the action of God among the people and institutions around them. The massive change of heart recorded in the second chapter of the Acts of the Apostles, the day when three thousand joined the nascent Christian movement in response to the preaching of Peter, might be an example of this. Certainly, Luke's account of the first council in Jerusalem, when the predominantly Jewish church had become aware that God's saving plan would also embrace the Gentiles without requiring their conversion to Judaism, illustrates a communal breakthrough of immense importance (Acts 15). That moment almost parallels Peter's conversion on the lake: the Spirit's net was being cast wider, in ever more unfamiliar waters.

A time of transition can be a time of conversion in which attitudes of heart and habits of mind undergo a radical change. The world no longer looks or feels the same, or so predictable, either to individuals or to groups. The old wineskins are simply incapable of holding the new wine, and people begin replacing them. Like Nicodemus, they realize that their natural expectations cannot go far enough to accommodate the breath of the Spirit. They need new categories in which to think and imagine. Seeing life with fresh clarity, or perhaps seeing things clearly for the first time in their lives, people might, like Zacchaeus, part with half of their fortunes (Lk 19:8).

For many people, Vatican II came to symbolize transition, conversion and renewal. The church, so ruggedly sure of itself, had suddenly come face-to-face with the modern world and discovered that God's concerns indeed went beyond matters of religion. To speak the word of God to men and women of today, it had first to listen to their experience: their joys and hopes, sorrows and anxieties. The church also needed to take a close, hard look at itself—its rituals, its dogmatism, its own anxieties and fears, its very way of being church—and search for the new wineskins. A world increasingly conscious of the misery and oppression endured by so many human beings needed both to understand the nature of those institutions and relationships which to a large degree had created such misery, and to discover solutions to liberate men and women. The God of the Christian tradition, the God of Jesus who was first and foremost the liberating God of Israel, was inseparable from the deepest, simplest aspirations of the world's poor. This God was therefore inseparably associated with the thirst for freedom felt everywhere around the globe where human beings suffered. And if God was associated with the thirst, God must also be intimately involved with those movements and forces that were working to change the usual way the world carried on its business.

Religion may have connected God with the churches, but the God of human life had drawn the churches to notice those locked in despair and anger within the neighborhoods of our inner cities, the landless poor who labored in the fields, the plantations, the mines and the factories, the chronically illiterate. The God who had "stirred" Cyrus, the "irreligious" Persian ruler, to restore the people of Israel, could just as well use any persons, group or movement—whether Christian or not—to liberate the world's poor from oppression.[2] The divine concern, after all, was not religion, but salvation. And that salvation had to comprise more than the saving of souls from eternal death. The power of sin and death destroyed life in this world, where human beings have bodies that can feel insult and hunger, where they have minds that can rot from ignorance and half-truths, and where despair and hatred cause their hearts to stop pulsing.

The longstanding battle for freedom and equality among blacks in South Africa may not appear religious, but it must be so, profoundly, because where men and women seek justice and dignity, there is the Spirit of God. The bloody struggle for a fair distribution of land and resources in Guatemala and El Salvador, or the desire of Palestinians for a homeland, may not appear religious, but that struggle and desire perhaps should be regarded this way, for the Spirit of God moves among them: "Blessed are the poor," the gospel tells us, and "Blessed are those who hunger and thirst for justice." The same point can be made about the labor movement in our own country, the pursuit of civil rights, the aspirations of women to be accorded the full measure of human dignity, the clamoring of minorities for equal opportunity. The thirst for freedom and justice is what links the various parts of the human family far more than any particular religious tradition, because what matters to God extends beyond the personal moral or religious sphere and reaches everything that plays a part in the humanization of the earth.[3]

The same impulse can be found in the countries of eastern Europe, among the Kurdish people in northern Iraq, and persecuted minorities everywhere on the planet. As the population of the world swells, we shall be observing ever larger migrations of people fleeing political oppression and bleak economies in search of a way of life which is both humane and secure. As one writer has put it:

> The citizens of well-to-do societies get a glimpse of the poverty in which millions are forced to live in television broadcasts of famine in (say) Ethiopia or in *National Geographic* magazine's photo-

graphs of slum cities in Latin America: the stricken landscape, the squalor, the attenuated limbs, the signs of disease, above all, the thousands and thousands of young children. If the sights are pitiful now, how will they seem when those regions possess three times as many human beings as today? . . . The issue of global demographic imbalances between richer and poorer societies forms the backdrop to all of the other important forces for change that are taking place.[4]

This natural desire for more humane living on the part of so many people will require a world order capable of meeting their aspirations. The prospect of a world where literally billions of people find themselves permanently frustrated and shut out from the resources of their planet is simply frightening. Where God will be in all of this should not be difficult to figure out. God will be with the peacemakers, at the side of those who hunger and thirst for justice, among those enduring the twin scourges of poverty and despair. To allow their voices, their faces and their aspirations into one's mind and imagination is to learn how to be present to God in the only way befitting a follower of Jesus.

2

Why Do Christians Sound So Dull?

It makes eminent sense that in a time of transition people will look to trusted institutions, ideas and ways of doing things in order to cope with their insecurity about where things are heading. If something has worked in the past, why does it need fixing? If the way we did things was good enough for my parents and grandparents, why should it not be good enough for me and my children? Besides, changing what does not need to be changed only confuses people. One gets used to doing things a certain way, reciting things a certain way, believing things a certain way. I have listened to adult Catholics complain about dismal preaching and dull eucharistic liturgies. Yet they continue to attend the liturgy, faithfully, perhaps because they have grown unalterably accustomed to the routine of going to church on Sundays. Somehow the routine creates a healthy distance for them from the ordinary pattern of activities and work, and helps to stabilize their lives in a world where peace, order and economic security seem so fragile. They simply need a "ritual break."

Needless to say, such a motive for going to church has little to do with the intrinsic meaning of the eucharist. Besides, it has been my experience that many young people never even reach the point of saying, "It worked well enough for my parents and grandparents." Instead, they are likely to argue, "It may have worked for my parents and grandparents, but it does absolutely nothing for me." What these young people readily admit becomes a vital reminder to all of us that the work of Vatican II remains unfinished. It would have been un-realistic to suppose that the immense task of updating the church could have been dispatched in the space of twenty-five or thirty years. Much of the vision and many of the hopes born from the council still remain unrealized.

One of the distressing signs of our times has been the emergence of emotional, charismatic or pentecostal sects among traditionally Catholic populations in Central and South America. I call their appearance distressing because the sects seem to imprison people with religion rather than set them free, the way Jesus would have done. Their way of presenting the gospel prevents poor people from realizing that they are being alienated from their own experience, in the way that the poor widow of the gospel story believed she was pleasing God by donating to the Temple treasury everything she had to live on, as if the God of Israel willed poor widows to go hungry. These evangelical groups promote "fervent spiritualism and a pro-capitalist ideology of hard work, sober living habits and individual advancement." According to some accounts, in the years following the council, the Catholic Church in Latin America opened itself to the concerns of liberation theology and made a preferential option for the poor. Referring to the situation in Brazil, one evangelical pastor observed, "The irony is that the Catholics opted for the poor, and the poor opted for the Evangelicals."[5]

Liberation theology has certainly had its share of critics. Some have accused it of being communist and fomenting class conflict, others have accused it of being anti-hierarchy, and still others have concluded that liberation theology must have been wrong-headed if the poor, finally, are deserting the Catholic tradition after all the fuss the church made about faith doing justice. Some contend that the theology of liberation had nothing to offer the poor in the way of genuine Christian spirituality.

Yet the fact that the poor are being drawn away by the evangelical sects can also be accounted for in another way: there simply have not been enough priests to meet their needs. Evangelical sects can set up a church overnight in an apartment, a storefront or an abandoned garage; I have seen the same thing happen in the neighborhood where I live. They are created from small groups of family, friends and neighbors: devout, enthusiastic, and usually poor. In such communities they find the inner strength and social support they need to survive.

But this phenomenon can hardly be attributed to the failure of

liberation theology. If anything, the appearance of the small evangelical churches fits in nicely with the concept of "base Christian communities," which have sprung up in various parts of Latin America, and
which correspond to the desire to belong to a faith community where
one feels personally supported and encouraged. Yet here the similarity
between the sects and the base communities ends. The creation of base
communities has been important to the empowerment of politically
and economically disenfranchised people. These communities are
small enough so that people can know and be concerned about one
another; they are lay-directed, well organized and steeped in the gospel. But they are concerned not only about religion, and certainly not
about religion conceived as a private affair between the individual and
God. The base Christian communities also have a vital stake in improving the quality of the lives of their members materially and socially,
and they are committed to pursuing those means required to bring that
change about in accordance with the gospel.

The theology of liberation provides a good example of something
new in the church, which has disturbed or frightened many. Indeed,
the pursuit of justice has revealed where the true conflict of our times
lies. The spiritually problematic issue identified by liberation theology
has never been the security offered by faith, but the security offered by
the status quo which invoked God and religion by way of ideological
defense. The pursuit of justice ran contrary to the vested interests of
economic and political institutions. Better to promote a different sort of
spirituality, one that embraces capitalist values, than to allow the poor
to be confused by Marxist thought disguised as the gospel!

Yet those who would urge that the church's option for the poor
should have been instead an option for an evangelical-style spirituality
entirely miss the point for several reasons. First, the pentecostal take-
over may itself amount to little more than a resubmitting to foreign
domination and a spirituality that impoverishes the gospel story by
spiritualizing and moralizing it. It is hardly accidental that fundamentalist movements in Guatemala, for example, received financial support from wealthy first-world donors.[6] The story of Jesus is actually
closer to the lives of those struggling to overcome poverty and powerlessness than most of the poor themselves realize. And secondly, what
stands in the way of there being greater church presence among the

poor is the church's own legislation (not the gospel's) that priests have to be male and celibate. The problem, in other words, is largely one of our own making, and it would be nonsense to pray that the Spirit bail us out of it. In short, the spirit of liberation theology, like the spirit of the council, has frequently been distrusted.

The theology of liberation represents an effort to rejoin the gospel and life, particularly the life of oppressed people. The gospel is very much a living story, and it also speaks to the experience of those who have been well-off because they have had the good fortune to be born in a first-world country. The gospel can speak to both rich and poor because the story of Jesus connects their respective histories: the salvation of the one depends upon the salvation of the other.

The dullness and boredom which young people attribute to the church may be traced to the fact that the culture around them is not sufficiently contemplative to allow them to develop a sense of God's presence and to learn how to pray. But the same excuse would not apply to those of us who are older, who likewise have found the religious forms weak on meaning, but who do not wish to renounce the weekly ritual of breaking away from the everyday world. If there is a deeper reason, then, for the lack of interest on the part of both young and old in the outward forms of religious observance, it may lie in the direction of a rupture within experience itself: the gospel has not been connected to life, in the way that the story of Jesus makes the salvation of the rich and the salvation of the poor inseparable.

The "life" referred to here is not simply *my* life, and the need is not simply *my* need to find personal spiritual meaningfulness in the gospel story. "Life" here has to do with the life we share together, because the same Spirit breathed it into each of us. So long as the life of any man or woman on the planet remains heavily burdened, everyone's life is incomplete.

Religious forms lose their meaning, not because they no longer have the power to console us. Rather, they lose their meaning when they are no longer in touch with the root metaphor of our faith. When Christians no longer think, act and pray in terms of the reign of God, their faith has lost its base. Some may hang on to the ritual and routine, because they do not have the time or interest to explore exotic religions of the east, and because there is something comforting about sameness and predictability. Others may let go of their religious tradition altogether because it failed to address their experience.

I am not concerned here with Christians who have become alienated from the church or from their religious heritage for other reasons. One understands the reaction of women who believe that their gifts for ministry have not been fully recognized by the church. One also understands the reaction of individuals who have been turned away from the church because of first-hand contact with the sad behavior of some priests. One might also appreciate the reaction of people put off by the authoritarian way in which the church sometimes functions. As understandable as these attitudes and reactions might be, they still do not get to the heart of things. The heart of the crisis is that the story of Jesus fails to speak to many people's experience because the experience itself is limited; it has not been enlarged by contact with the experience of people at the bottom or at the edge of society.

We cannot blame the story itself for what has happened. The problem is that too few really know the story fully, and can tell it faithfully, with enthusiasm. Fidelity to the story requires that we tell it in a way that never lets the salvation of the rich be torn away from the salvation of the poor. It must talk about Jesus without ever allowing the import of the reign of God to slip from view.

Why do Christians sound so dull? This is more than a question of dull liturgies (we have all experienced these, clergy and laity alike). This is also more than a matter of uninspiring sermons (I have delivered my share of these, too). Nor is the point that Christians, as Christians, have little to talk about except church matters or pious practices. The only thing some people expect from religion is consolation, assurance and peace. While such expectations are understandable, one should not hope to find them by meditating on the story of Jesus. And if that is all one wants, then Christian faith is going to be very dull.

But if a person wants to live out of the gospel story, with a vision of the future formed through meditation on the reign of God, then that individual's conversation and life are going to be animated by hope. The story of Jesus adds vibrancy and enthusiasm to prayer, and it makes being human something almost charismatic: to live for others, with faith in the God of the poor. Men and women living out of the gospel story are examples of humanity redeemed and liberated. They are people capable of living for others, they are intensely interested in the wider world, and they realize that the work of God is the liberation of human beings from the forces of poverty and oppression. People living out of the gospel story are anything but bored with the things of God.

3

Of Trials and Projects

The Uruguayan Jesuit theologian, Juan Luis Segundo, drew attention to the difference between salvation conceived as a trial and salvation conceived as a project: not so much our project but God's.[7] The religious perspective (it would even be fair to describe it as a religious "myth") which most of us inherited was that we were placed on this earth as a test of our willingness to resist temptation, do "meritorious" acts and grow in charity. If we advanced in virtue by successfully enduring this vale of tears, then we would pass into the reward of eternal life. The present world is but a shadow; real existence lies in another, unseen world.

Viewing human existence as a trial leads to an extremely individualistic approach to salvation, as we have already seen. It also undercuts the value of whatever plans and works we set our hands to here, as we conceive and build a better world for ourselves and our children. Such a perspective, in other words, fails to draw any connection between the work in which we spend our lives and our piety or faith. Human labor becomes simply instrumental, a necessary means to an end: one works merely in order to survive.

Salvation conceived as a project, on the other hand, looks to human beings as collaborating with God in the fashioning of the world. The divine project is nothing less than the full creation of human beings and their communities within a world which is truly humanizing, a world wherein men and women are free to develop as God's daughters and sons. What would things be like, we might ask ourselves, if the Spirit of God reigned in human thinking, deciding and acting? To live one's life, to plan one's future and to imagine the world in terms of the divine project becomes, for the Christian, the centering aim of our heart, soul, mind and strength. Human labor and energy thus play an integral role in the realization of the divine project: the reign of God will not arrive unless we open ourselves up to it by actively participating in its coming into being. Patience, endurance and suffering, which are obviously aspects of our experience, must be framed or interpreted in terms of the reign of God: we suffer and endure setbacks, resistance, failure and humiliation for the sake of the project to which we have dedicated our lives. We bear the exhaustion and fatigue of hard work because the earth will not be both a humanized and humanizing place unless men and women do their utmost to accomplish this.

Segundo's helpful clarification reflects an important insight within liberation theology that can likewise be found in the christological work of other Latin American writers. The story of Jesus, too, can be read in terms of trial and project. The "trial" reading portrays redemption as the work that Jesus must suffer as the eternally designated servant of God. Through what he suffered, Jesus learned obedience; by successfully enduring the test of his passion and death, Jesus was awarded "the name that is above every name" (Phil 2:9).

Yet not only is Jesus rewarded for his virtue; his suffering or "trial" became the cause of our salvation as well. Exactly why God would have connected Jesus' trial with our redemption remains unclear. On this showing, the salvation of the world seems to be the result of a private arrangement between God and Jesus and does not actively involve us. The net result is that the story of Jesus becomes the prototype of a life on trial: he was sent into the world to endure the cross, and thereby to provide us a model of how we should learn the same patient obedience through the things which we must undergo.

When the story of Jesus is told in a way that makes the reign of God the linchpin holding all its details together we have the life of Jesus viewed as project. Again, the overarching project is God's cause conceived as the full integration of human beings, or as their full liberation from everything which oppresses and dehumanizes them. In other words, God wills human wholeness.[8] This project is not something which only a few chosen individuals, like prophets and saints, are called to share in. God's project embraces all of us, and the invitation to immerse oneself in it is likewise addressed to all.

The specifically evangelical nature of suffering and endurance arises from its connection with the reign of God. Or, to put matters a little differently, diminishment and pain are permanent features of human existence. The Buddha, for example, five centuries before Jesus, became a savior figure who instructed his followers on how they might escape suffering through meditation and asceticism. But the gospel story is not about *coping* with sickness, pain, violence or injustice. The story of Jesus does not provide us with a spirituality of suffering, nor does it automatically confer upon suffering some sort of transcendental value. The Christian tradition, as we have seen, developed a mysticism of the cross along those lines; but that was not the purpose of Jesus' passion and death. The cross of Jesus emerged as the consequence of his dedication to God's project, and anyone who answers the invitation to join in that project is implicitly opening himself or herself to the same possibility. The pain which results from living for the reign of God is peculiarly or specifically evangelical: the cross does not symbolize *all* the suffering and misery of the human condition, but only that which the reign of God exacts of those who spend their lives for their sisters and brothers.

Segundo's clarification confirms once more the importance of knowing the story of Jesus. If we ask where we are to get our bearings in this time of transition, then the first point might well be the gospel story. Modern biblical scholarship has enabled us to retrieve major elements of that story: the Jewishness of Jesus, his humanness and his faith. Furthermore, it has helped us to understand who Jesus was (and is) by viewing him in relationship to the reign of God rather than in terms of some secret identity. Although it may sound odd to phrase things this way, we need to remind ourselves that Jesus has to be centered in terms of the God of Israel, not vice versa. Jesus was a messenger of the reign of God; his identity derives from his mission or work. We have to move away from thinking that whatever Jesus said and taught gained its importance from the fact that it was Jesus, the Son of God, who said and did such things. God's aim was not to display Jesus to the world but, through him, to make all men and women sharers in the divine promise.

The people of Israel may have thought that the promise was uniquely theirs, and that the God of the heavens and the earth was

Israel's God. But the God of Israel never ceased to be the God of all the nations. The God of Israel was the God of the Gentiles, too, even if they were not fully aware of this. The reign of God would not be only Israel's gift; it was to be offered to all peoples. Jesus' "sonship"—who he was—is inseparable from that mission.

By endeavoring to unlock the secret of his identity in terms of a unique relationship with God which can only be spelled out speculatively and by recourse to philosophical categories, we miss the mark. It cannot be that the only truly orthodox ones among us will be speculative theologians, since they are the only group that can grasp the subtleties, distinctions and intricacies of Christian belief about "two natures in one person" or "three persons in one God." If this were so, the vast majority of us would be left with no touchstone of orthodoxy other than our subscribing to a precise verbal formula within the creed. This would blow verbal (and conceptual) orthodoxy out of all proportion, and leave people wondering what the doctrinal fuss has been all about. Perhaps the orthodox answer to questions about Jesus and his relationship with God lies in the way that we tell the story.

In addition, perhaps too much has been made of Jesus' "*Abba* experience." By attending to how Jesus addressed God, or referred to God, as "Father," one then proceeded to imagine what being Son meant and speculate about Jesus' identity rather than explore his faith. What matters to us is the faith of Jesus, and the religious experience within which he knew God, since that is the experience we have been called to share in. That experience enables us to understand better what Jesus meant by the reign of God; it does not enable us to penetrate the metaphysics of the "divine nature" and how Jesus came to possess it.

We would not be exaggerating things by insisting that the future of the church, the believing community, lies in the hands of its storytellers. It is no doubt true that, following the council, people experienced all sorts of dislocations as various changes were introduced. Still, in themselves those changes were minor: a change in language, a change in the position of the eucharistic table, a simplification of rituals, the creation of parish councils, and so forth. The effect of such changes, however, was to awaken people's awareness of the changeability of an institution that had presented itself as beyond change. It awakened

Know, understand, love, follow [handwritten annotation]

them to the difference between the institution's rhetoric and its practice. It demonstrated that even the church was not impervious to great
historical currents, and that however much it resisted, the church
could not isolate itself from a world that harbored democratic aspirations: aspirations which would touch the church itself. In short, the
changes were small, but the message they delivered went beyond anything we could immediately perceive.

Nevertheless, the lasting fruit of the council was not that Catholics should find themselves unsettled, unsure of what to believe, or
unnerved by the changeability (and the fallibility) of the church. The
fruit was that the council sent the church back to its sources, back to its
beginning in the gospel story; for it is to the gospels that the church had
to look to recover its charism. Catholics had finally realized what the
world around them knew only too well, namely, that no one stands
above history. History penetrates everything about us. Rituals, symbols, doctrines, laws, customs, structures of governance and administra-
tion: none of these things stands above history in a timeless zone
immune from change. Yet in going back to the gospels, the church
would not discover there the timeless foundation that could legitimate
the way it had done business for nearly twenty centuries. The gospels
themselves could not stand above history; indeed, the gospels, too,
were a product of time and place and circumstance. To know Jesus one
had to know his times; to understand Jesus, one had to understand his
Jewish roots. To love Jesus one also had to love the human race, and to
follow Jesus one had to open oneself to the reign of God.

In short, there is no bedrock upon which to build a lasting city.
Buildings, cultures, civilizations come and go. There is no decisive,
unambiguous divine intervention in history that might serve as a fixed
platform in a sea of change. There is no institution that can boast
immunity against the forces of history. When all is said and done, what
we fall back on is the story, which is also our story, because now we
have become actors within it. The gospel story is about God's project in
the world, told within the ordinariness and particularity of village life
in first-century Palestine. The Galilean countryside in which Jesus
walked and spoke provides the imaginative framework within which we
find the meanings, the critical scenes and encounters, from which we
can re-view our own world. We have chosen to stay with that story, to

deepen our grasp of it and to pass it along to the next generation, because in that story we have discovered life. Indeed, we have discovered our own lives. But even more importantly, in the gospel we have found the story of God and the great project of liberating the world from sin and oppression. In a time of transition, the first place we turn to is the story. In the story, we remember who we are.

Families have been known to pass along stories of relatives long since deceased, their adventures (or misadventures), because memories of our ancestors are both important and precious. These help us to identify ourselves and to distinguish us from other families; the past is no longer felt as an obscure mist out of which we suddenly and miraculously emerged. The stories map our beginnings and create our sense of really belonging to history. The only requirement for stepping into the world of these stories is that we belong to, or in the case of in-laws and close friends, that we want to be accepted as part of the family. Apart from this sense of being or belonging to family, the stories might not be nearly so interesting.

The same thing holds true for the stories from our religious tradition. They interest us only to the degree that we have invested ourselves in the life of the community. The biblical stories are not the only stories that engage us, of course; there have been many other stories added to these over the centuries. The Jesuit tradition to which I belong recounts proudly the great mission stories involving the first members of the Society to work in China and their pioneering efforts at adapting European Christianity to eastern culture, and the bold pastoral work among the Guarani in Paraguay which was the subject of the film *The Mission*. But the biblical stories, and particularly the gospel, hold pride of place among all the stories of faith. The obvious point here needs to be underlined, however: stories will interest us to the degree that we have a stake in the community. If we actually feel that we belong to a community of believers (and are not merely "members" on a roll of churchgoers), or if we want to belong to the believing community, then the memories which have been handed down to us acquire the power to pull us into the circle of faith.

I would even go one step farther. The presupposition for being interested by and in the Christian stories of Jesus is a sense of belonging to the whole human family, or at least of wanting to be accepted as part of that larger community. Apart from this, our interest in the stories and memories of the whole people of God will be more notional and academic than real and immediate. The reason, for example, that a person might be interested in the great stories from the Hebrew scriptures, or Old Testament, is that these are memories handed on by men and women of faith which narrate their experience of God active in our world. I do not believe that such stories derive their attractiveness from the fact that they formed part of Jesus' cultural and religious heritage, and for that (indirect) reason they become of interest to us.

Again, the presupposition for appreciating those stories, and the stories and memories enshrined in the religious and cultural traditions and sacred writings of all peoples, is that we have a lively sense of belonging to the great human family. I am interested, for example, in the story of God's appearance to Moses and the deliverance of the Israelites from slavery, because this is a memory which inserts me into the historical experience not only of Israel, but of all peoples which have suffered under tyranny and exile. Yet the same instinct leads me to listen to the stories of the Incas and the Mayas, for the descendants of these peoples live among us; and I am equally interested in the stories handed on by native Americans and black Americans. Once one sees oneself related to all these people as family, then one does not want to be ignorant of his or her family history.

There are limits, of course, to what any one individual can do in a lifetime. Nevertheless, the basic point holds true. The stories of faith, like the stories from our parents and grandparents, become interesting to us at that point in our lives when we feel that we really want to, and actually do, belong to a family. When we really want to, and realize that we actually do, belong to a family of believers, then the stories about Jesus take on enormous significance and power. But things do not stop there, for in and through his story one is led to the wider human family and the history of the one people of God. Christian spirituality in the future will not be content to know and tell only Jesus' story. It will certainly do this, but it will also remain keenly alert to stories of God and God's people, to humanity's "scriptures," from whatever corner they might come.

4

Eucharist and Cross:
Abiding Signs of Solidarity

To suggest that Christian spirituality in the future will take its principal bearings from the story of Jesus is hardly to state something revolutionary or unexpected. The hidden issue here, however, lies in the question, "But whose version of the story?" And the answer is, "The story of Jesus as told through the experience of the poor, because first and foremost Jesus' story is really all about the struggle for their deliverance." It is not enough to uncover (or recover) the humanness of Jesus, something which many first-world theologians have endeavored to do. One must also recover the fact that this human Jesus was one of the victims in humanity's ongoing struggle for justice.

By rendering Jesus' human features clearly, theology has brought him closer to us. At the same time, by drawing attention to the tyrannies which governed the political, social and economic situation of his time, theology has distanced Jesus from the world and the experience of those of us who have been extremely fortunate in comparison with two-thirds of our fellow human beings. In short, the retelling of the story of Jesus creates a singular challenge for the Nicodemuses and Zacchaeuses among us. Zacchaeus was the wealthy individual who suddenly "clicked" on the message of Jesus and became aware of the misery his greed had caused to so many people (his story appears in Lk 19:1–10). Nicodemus was the devout, reflective individual who came to Jesus by night, to inquire further about his teaching, because he was puzzled about how the Spirit could remake someone whose outlook and outreach had become stale and narrow (see Jn 3:1–10). To these figures we might append the rich young man who was eager to follow

Jesus, until he learned of the cost (Mt 19:16–22). Or the earnest scribe (Matthew identified him as a lawyer) who questioned Jesus about the greatest commandment, and was surprised to find out that he already knew the correct answer (Mk 12:28–34).

In many ways, these people were similar to us: well-to-do, well-meaning, and at least *capable* of conversion. They remind us that no one need remain fixed (or imprisoned) in his or her present way of thinking, acting and believing. All of us can change. All of us can learn to transfer our loyalties to the whole people of God, especially to those who cry daily to God for bread, for fairness and for deliverance. The "preferential option for the poor," which is another way of describing this conversion, is not prompted primarily by guilt, although I believe it is almost impossible for those of us who have been richly blessed to behold the rest of the world without registering some feelings of guilt over the discrepancy that exists between rich and poor. The poor family living next door may be separated from us by an ocean, a continent or a national boundary, but they are every bit as truly our neighbor. Sometimes guilt can be a healthy response when one sits down to eat and notices through the window the barren table of the family living beside us.

The process in which our loyalties are reversed and in which we begin to make a preferential option for the poor can be somewhat complex. The moment of conversion may occur all at once, or it may unfold over a period of time. In either case, I believe that what initiates the process is not so much a theoretical consideration of the gospel's teaching but a discerning encounter with human misery, poverty and injustice. We meet people and we leave ourselves open to them. We see their condition, and we ask ourselves, "Why has this happened?" Instead of allowing the defensive gates around our feelings and preconceived ideas to slam shut, we make ourselves notice the world of the poor.

The insistence on the part of contemporary religious writers to force the "preferential option" to explicit awareness among all of us is not occasioned by resentment or a lingering hatred of the rich simply because they have means. Rather, these writers are simply attempting to spell out for their day the implications of Jesus' proclamation to repent and put our faith in the "good news."[9]

This leads, then, to the second point by which Christian spirituality must take its bearings. The customary pillars of the church's life are word (or story) and sacrament, narrative and symbol. If meditating on that word and those symbols, and bringing them to life, are what constitute theological reflection, then some measure of personal engagement in humanity's struggle to overcome the dehumanizing forces of sin provides the context for that reflection. Indeed, it sets the stage for all Christian prayer, which includes the community's liturgical celebrations. In short, the believing community can neither think nor pray authentically, that is, in the Spirit of Jesus, apart from personal involvement in the critical struggles of our time against the tyrannies of injustice.

How each one of us personally engages in these will depend upon a number of factors over which we have no control, such as our age, together with the physical and emotional energy available to us, or the responsibilities we may have toward husbands, wives and children. Nevertheless, the following of Jesus is going to pit us squarely against those whose interests, decisions and actions contribute to massive suffering. Indeed, following Jesus is going to introduce us to sisters and brothers whom we have never met, but whose voices and faces may cross our television screens, whose stories and pictures appear in our newspapers, and whose cries can pierce the most private areas of our minds and hearts.

The second point, then, is sacrament. And since the quintessential liturgical celebration is the eucharist, it is to the Lord's table that we must look in order to take our bearings. How we view the eucharist depends upon what we know about the story of Jesus. If the only thing that we remember is that Jesus ate a Passover meal with his disciples on the night before he died, then we may fall into thinking that the eucharist is primarily and exclusively intended to be a recollection of the death of Jesus, viewed as an offering to take away the sin of the world. It is no doubt true that the church's memory of the "last" supper was conditioned by its association with the cross, but it would be misleading to think that the death of Jesus brought about divine forgiveness. The mystery which unfolded on the cross included a disclosure of God's unconquerable love for the world; but, as we have already noted, the God of Israel had always been known and believed in as a God of mercy and compassion. Otherwise, Israel's prayers would have been meaningless:

> Have mercy on me, O God, according to your steadfast love;
>   according to your abundant mercy blot out my transgressions.
> Wash me thoroughly from my iniquity,
>   and cleanse me from my sin (Ps 51:1–2).

What the cross may have revealed was Jesus' own readiness to forgive, even under such horrible circumstances, those who had put him to death: "Father, forgive them; for they do not know what they are doing" (Lk 23:34). No matter how forcefully and angrily Jesus denounced those who abused other men and women, and contributed to their oppression, he never surrendered his capacity to behold *all* of the people as children of God.

Yet it was above all in Jesus' readiness to face death for the sake of the reign of God, for the sake of God's people, into whose struggle he had thrown himself, that we discover the harsh mystery of love. Jesus' love, like God's, could embrace all. But there was a condition: human beings had to open themselves to that love through conversion, or through a humble acknowledgment of their need for God's mercy and grace. However, if they refused, if they blocked the word of God by selfishness and greed, or by arrogance and the pursuit of privilege, then the only recourse was to the power of suffering itself. Sometimes, when we are forced to look at what terrible destruction our sin causes, we may be stunned into conversion.[10]

But I suspect that the power of the cross as a symbol derives from the fact that there the believer catches sight of all the "crucified" people of the world in humanity's struggle against injustice and enslavement. There, on the cross, Jesus hangs in solidarity with his people. Christian devotion toward the cross has been more or less predetermined by the way the story of Jesus has been told to us. Beholding the crucified Jesus, the believer responds by declaring his or her own sinfulness and begging for forgiveness. The story of Jesus has been reduced to God's being reconciled to the world through the death of his Son. It may be, however, that the ones from whom forgiveness is to be sought are the poor, all the victims in humanity's age-old struggle, and not the crucified Jesus. If that is the case, then Jesus' disposition, recorded in the words "Father, forgive them, for they do not know what they are doing," must be listened to as the voice of the poor themselves. And it is possible to hear these words issuing from them only at the moment when those who have crucified them become aware of what they have done. The crucified Jesus, in other words, is not a model of pious behavior but a vivid representation of the actual condition of most people in the world. The words of Jesus are not spoken for our edification, but to elicit a response, a declaration of one's own complicity in the destruction of innocent life. It is not so much to God, therefore, that we turn to for forgiveness, but to the sisters and brothers whom we have offended.

To the poor and oppressed themselves, the cross delivers a different message. It speaks of God's oneness with them in their experience. The cross, for them, is not an instrument of conversion but a call to resistance that never forgets against whom one is fighting. The oppressor ever remains their sister or their brother: it is this truth which gives rise to the tearful realization that the human tragedy, from God's eyes, is far more hurtful than most of us could ever fathom.

The notion of reconciliation which has been attached to the cross ought not to be understood in the first place as a matter of our being reconciled to God; being reconciled with God may prove to be the consequence of something else. What the cross opens up in the first place is the possibility of human beings being reconciled with one another. The cross confronts the privileged and powerful ones of this world with the enormous discrepancy between them and the others. It exposes the treachery of prestige and wealth, and all those forces that make it possible for one human being to lord it over another. The cross points them in the direction of their neighbor. For the poor and oppressed, the cross opens up a different possibility. They are brought face-to-face with a love and a loyalty that refuses to abandon them in their historical struggle. At the same time, the cross speaks to them of the only way that human relationships and social structures can finally be transformed. Apart from love, the world will always be at war. The poor are the ones, finally, who carry this word of God into history: they are the bearers of the promise. It is they who must convert the rich.

These remarks on the cross have been necessary in order to grasp the connection between the death of Jesus and the eucharist. The cross does not stand as an isolated event, liturgically memorialized in the church through the eucharist. Just as we need to keep the whole of Jesus' ministry in view as we look at the cross (for the whole of his life is summed up there), so too must we keep the whole of Jesus' ministry in mind as we try to explain what the eucharist means. We need to situate the last supper in this wider context, if we are going to celebrate it faithfully.

An Open Table

The most remarkable feature about the gospel's recollection of the numerous meals that Jesus shared with various people is the openness of the table. To sit at table with someone, or with some group, indicates a basic human receptiveness. If we refuse to sit at table with someone, then we are either calling attention to a serious breach between us, or we are refusing to tolerate something about that individual's thinking or behavior. The "righteous" people found many reasons not to sit down with certain individuals: they had not bathed, or they were not churchgoers, or they engaged in forbidden professions. They might have been poor, or maimed, or unsightly, or Gentiles, or tax-collectors, or prostitutes, or ritually defiled, or just too ordinary. Jesus' admonition to his well-to-do host

> "When you give a luncheon or a dinner, do not invite your friends or your brothers or your relatives or rich neighbors, in case they may invite you in return, and you would be repaid. But when you give a banquet, invite the poor, the crippled, the lame, and the blind. And you will be blessed, because they cannot repay you" (Lk 14:12–14)

could well serve as an instruction to a community about the meaning of its eucharistic celebration. The Lord's table is by definition open to all: that is its purpose. To recall Jesus at table, therefore, is to remember him in his being open and accepting of all, but especially of his being open and accepting of those outside the law, those of little means, those disesteemed by the respectable ones of society. Having a meal with Jesus thus became a premier sign of the reign of God. The reign of God is like a feast where all have been invited; unfortunately, some have declined, especially once they discovered who else was on the guest list.

Apparently, many people took offense at Jesus' habit of meal-taking. By accepting people so readily into his company he was, in effect, saying that one sure way to achieve reconciliation with God is through being reconciled with one's sisters and brothers. And what more effective way to do this than to recline at table and break bread with one another? If divine pardon could be realized so easily, then the rituals of religion clearly assumed a very secondary role in Jesus' piety and thinking. The table of any family, insofar as it strived to be open to all, could become a place of reconciliation and forgiveness. The effective measure of this openness was an individual's, or a family's, readiness to welcome the marginalized of society to its table. For the poor, this might not have posed so great a problem as it would have for the righteous and the well-to-do. Still, the basic structure of forgiveness was clear. Something so simple and ordinary as breaking bread together could be a channel of divine mercy and blessing.

The fact that the gospel recalls the occasions of Jesus being at table should not lead us to think that forgiveness could occur only when he was present. Indeed, he set an example; but any household which welcomed the outcasts had already done what God required in order to be righteous in God's sight. What the community did, however, was to "include" Jesus every time they ate together. Jesus was "present" at all the meals, in every family and household, shared by Jesus' companions and followers. He was the ever-present guest; even the simplest table would become the Lord's table. And, once again, the only condition upon his being really present in the homes of his followers was their readiness to accept all. Obviously, it would have been impossible for all the poor, all the marginalized people, literally to sit down at table. No table would have been large enough, no family wealthy enough (let alone the families of those who had very little to share) to accommodate everyone in need. But that was not the point. What mattered was a person's readiness to accept others, one's openness to recognizing those in need as one's neighbor—to be loved in the same way we love ourselves. The eucharist became associated with forgiveness, therefore, not because of its association with the cross, but because of its connection with all the meals of Jesus' life. The cross thus appears as the price Jesus paid for the company he kept at dinner.[11]

This holds enormous implications for the Christian practice of celebrating the Lord's supper. Christian spirituality is rightly centered on both word and sacrament, but sacrament is not merely a ritual detached from the wider world in which we live. That wider world provides the context within which we think and pray, worship and celebrate. In the measure that our liturgical prayer keeps that wider world in view, and in the measure that we bring that wider world of human experience with us when we gather for our eucharists, the liturgy itself will prove to be lifegiving. The prayers we recite, the reflections we make, the rituals and gestures we employ: all of these must be focused in terms of the whole story of Jesus.

At the end of his recent study of the eucharist, David Power writes:

> Liturgy finally leads to doxology and contemplation, in the communion with Christ at his table. As participation in his mystery it must be authenticated by the community's testimony. In that sense, liturgy is never its own justification. It does not establish its own truth. It is verified by the practice of the beatitudes and the solidarity with the suffering of those who proclaim Jesus as Lord. . . . The orthodoxy of the eucharistic canon is verified by the orthopraxis of solidarity with victims and with those who hope and serve the fullness of human life, even in the midst of suffering and injustice.[12]

The openness of Christ's table is demonstrated through the way Christians practice their faith. And because the eucharist is the community's remembering Jesus as a victim, as someone who was drawn into the history of oppression, the practice of faith is going to be measured above all in terms of the community's oneness with the Jesus who still suffers in the poor and defenseless. But this cannot be a sterile, invisible oneness. Sharing at Christ's table disposes us for action and service; oneness with Christ is shown above all in the way that we live for others: this is the testimony Power speaks about. Yet, how would we know what the bread and cup signify, apart from the story which gives them their meaning? What justification would the church have for linking the breaking of bread and the sharing of a cup with the breaking of Jesus and the spilling of his blood, apart from the history of sin and oppression which had claimed him? If our eucharistic worship does not help us to remember this, then the table would no longer be Christ's.

5

How Shall We Pray?

Many people like to pray through their imaginations; I do. In reading the gospels, for example, they imagine Jesus in the various scenes interacting with people: speaking, healing, sharing a meal, walking through the countryside of Galilee and Judea, and instructing his disciples. As a result, through the power of imagination, they become present to those scenes, and Jesus becomes present to them. Needless to say, the believing community recognized an important difference between a person's presence to Jesus through imagination, framed in terms of the events and settings provided for us by the evangelists, and the risen, living Jesus whom it also referred to as Christ and Lord. No matter how human and rooted in the earth Jesus might be, as re-created through the power of imagination, the one to whom the believer intentionally relates is the living Lord. Indeed, as we have already seen, the real direction of prayer is always God-ward. Thus we speak and relate to Jesus as we would to God, because for us Jesus—the risen Christ—has become an icon or sacrament of God's presence.

In order for that prayer relationship to be genuinely Christian, that is, founded in the Spirit of Jesus, a person needs to know the story of Jesus. In addition, prayer which is properly Christian also needs to be rooted in a community of believers whose table is open to the least ones among us. The mystery of reconciliation is first and foremost the coming together of men and women who are, before all else, sisters and brothers. Identifying and dismantling the structures, prejudices and economic arrangements that keep brothers and sisters divided is a most concrete expression of what the gospel means by the forgiveness of sins. If, with the help of God and following the example of Jesus, we can sit at table together, then the grace of reconciliation will have been realized. And until the barriers are torn down, the great feast cannot take place. The Lord's supper will mark the mutual forgiveness of those who have been converted; but many seats will remain empty, until the prodigal ones return home, until the disgruntled older brothers come inside, until the resistant ones run out of excuses, until the rich and righteous change their ways. The Lord's table reveals an already and a not-yet, gratitude for what is and eager longing for what can still be.

But is there a style of prayer appropriate to a spirituality in transition? Many people find that the prayers they were taught and memorized as children are hopelessly inadequate to satisfy their growing thirst for an adult relationship with God. This is not the place to discuss the notion of wordless or nondiscursive prayer, the simple prayer of quiet or prayer of the heart. For some people today, however, the very activity of praying is disorienting. They are not sure what they are doing, to whom they are speaking, and why they should be pressured into prayer in the first place. They have grown beyond the point of speaking to God as one friend might speak to another. For them, God is beyond words; God cannot be objectified the way a person sitting in front us is. The more they think about what they are actually doing, the more bewildered and frustrated they become. What is the difference between a person talking to himself, or even to a make-believe companion, out loud in an empty room, and a person speaking to God in solitude? Would we call the first person insane and the second person a saint? Is the difference merely the fact that, as everybody knows, the imaginary companion is purely a product of fantasy, while God is eminently "real"? And that so long as a person intends to be in touch with the real, he or she actually is? Clearly, prayer has to mean more than that.

However we arrive there, prayer at its deepest level is a relationship with God which is both conscious and pervasive. One may not always be explicitly aware of God, but God is certainly within one's horizon of awareness. In the same way, a wife might not always be thinking about her husband, or a husband about his wife; but the spouse—the loved one—has a permanent presence within the other's mind and heart. The actual time they spend together, intimately conversing and sharing, may be quite small compared to what they do during the rest of their days and weeks. But, at least in the ideal order,

How naming moves our prayer

they never cease being present to one another, concerned about one another, in love with one another, even when that presence, concern and love are mediated by raising and caring for children, or by the need to work in order to support the family, or even by the ways they take proper care of themselves precisely so that their relationship can be enriched.

But God is not a person the way a husband or wife is. That is why people often pray to God through the saints. The mind's eye can picture the form of Mary, or Jesus, one of the saints, or even someone close to us who has died; but it cannot picture God. We may call God "Father," but does any image or form appear in our minds? We believe that God is Love; but how does one pray to "love"? Even if we think of such difficulties, most of us probably never lose any sleep over them. We continue to pray, realizing that the whole business of prayer doesn't quite make sense in some ways, because reaching out to God is something that the human heart does spontaneously, even when God cannot be pictured or named.

This is not how we start out, of course. We start with simple prayers, already formulated. We imagine God as a super-parent, because we have been told that God is our "almighty Father." Yet as the years pass, and as we internalize both the Christian story and Christian practice, our view of God transcends the duality which characterizes a child's approach to God. There is an "us"; but there is no "God and me." God does not stand apart, or even alongside, as one human being accompanies another. We know beyond any doubt that we are not God, yet we cannot think of ourselves alone, either, because somehow the mystery of God has been stitched into the fabric of our souls. There is Another, whose creative hands hold all things in heaven and on earth.

I have watched teenagers, whose mothers or fathers left them when they were youngsters, become intensely interested in learning the whereabouts of the absent parent. The fact that the mother or father walked out on them leaves them vulnerable and often deeply, frighteningly angry; yet the possibility that maybe they could still have that ideal relationship with their father or mother which they crave drives them to search for the missing love. Observing this leaves me sad, because their searching always end in disappointment. The ideal relationship will not exist for them. Yet in this there may lie a parable. I wonder sometimes whether the real reason for a lot of human anger might not be the absence of God from people's lives; I mean, their not really knowing God, or their missing a clear relationship with the one who made them. Many human beings spend their lives unconsciously searching for the absent parent.

Now, I doubt that Jesus ever went through this experience of searching: not because Jesus never had to ponder over what God was like, or wrestle over whether God could be trusted, but because Jesus was not abandoned by his parents. Thus he bore no residual anger toward life; for him, "the Father" did not serve as a refuge because he never knew the full love and support of a human family. If we look to the life of Jesus in order to find a paradigm for the human being's growth in prayer, then we shall be disappointed. Jesus' prayer life most likely developed as he grew and matured humanly in wisdom and grace, but we do not know enough about his prayer to be able to follow, let alone propose, any ascent into mysticism. The gospel writers were not concerned about writing an ascetical treatise on the life of prayer and meditation, and while he was remembered as a devout man, Jesus was not remembered as a world-transcending mystic, but as a prophet.

The word "contemplation" has to do with seeing, but contemplative prayer is by no means something passive. In contemplative prayer, a person is pulled outside of himself or herself into a different world, a different way of looking at reality, or a different set of concerns. Above all, the concerns which capture and hold one's attention are God's own concerns. But what else would God be concerned about, except human beings: and not simply human beings in general, equally, universally and without any distinctions, but particularly human beings whose cries for deliverance reach God's ears, and whose suffering and hunger God already knows. The practical result of contemplative prayer is action on behalf of others.

To put the point another way, maybe it is the poor and the oppressed who pull prayer out of us. We pray, not just because praying is a sound thing for creatures to do. Prayer is not merely one of the responsibilities we assume for being a creature, or for being a Christian; it ought not to be portrayed as a debt we must render to God. What we do owe God is obedience to the "way of life" (see Deut 30:15–20). That is, attendant upon the fact that we are creatures is the requirement that we act justly and treat one another with the same respect and high regard out of which God has created and treated us. In order to be able to live and act as God expects, with justice and compassion, we must know how to pray. But who will teach us, not so much to recite the right words to God, but to view the world with burning concern for its needs and its woundedness? Who will pull from our hearts those wordless cries for peace and justice, or those angry protests against barbaric disregard for the dignity of life? Who will point us God-ward, so that we pray as we should, namely, in union with the whole people of God? By letting ourselves be drawn into the suffering of the poor, we shall know, perhaps for the first time, how to address God.

The renowned Benedictine monk, Bede Griffiths, spent much of his life in an ashram in India, where he found himself bridging the faith he had been steeped in as a western Christian, and the spirituality of a predominantly Hindu culture. Griffiths had tapped into the contemplative richness of the Asian religions, and suggested that in the future Christian faith could be vastly enriched through its conversation with the religions of the east.[13] Anyone who has spent time in the Far East and paid close attention to its religiousness could not help but be struck by the important role which meditation plays in the eastern search for the Spirit. Of course, all this was underscored by the spiritual probings of Thomas Merton, especially in the few years before he died, in the middle of his Asian journey. And Karl Rahner, speculating on the church of the future, predicted that Christians of the future would have to be mystics.[14]

While I do not wish to discount these signs of the times, and while I do not wish to ignore the potential richness in the confluence of eastern and western spiritual traditions, it is worth recalling that Jesus was not a guru, or a Zen master, or a spiritual director. He did not have disciples the way a skilled monk might have novices. In fact, the word "disciple" itself may be misleading. Philosophers and teachers in the Greco-Roman world had "disciples," and the evangelists, writing in Greek, turned those who "followed" Jesus into "disciples."[15] The word could lead us to construe the gospel dynamic in terms of a seminar room, whereas Jesus, the prophet from Galilee (who obviously was regarded by some as a rabbi or teacher) was not instructing people about philosophy and mathematics, history and rhetoric, but about the reign of God. And the only qualifications he had for this were his faith in the God of Israel and his experience. Besides, the gospel tells us that Jesus "called" his followers, whereas it was the prospective disciples of the philosophers who took the initiative in approaching their would-be teachers for acceptance into their circle.

Perhaps we need to look in a different direction in order to understand the contemplative dimension of the prayer which is properly Christian. Clearly, the practice of prayer, like any other human exercise or pursuit, will develop through that very practice. Furthermore, it should not be surprising that observers will discover affinities as they look from one religious tradition to another. The growth in the habit of prayer as the soul exercises itself by meditation should not be vastly different between east and west: the end result is hearts and minds transformed by compassion, liberation of spirit, and a transcendence of the world. If Jesus had withdrawn to the wilderness and passed his entire life there, then he might have acquired the self-dispossessed posture of the Buddha in meditation, or the lean features of a third-century anchorite. He might even have bequeathed to us his insight into the human spirit's gradual ascent to perfection.

But that is not what happened. We do better to review the histories of Israel's prophets in their passionate engagement with the word of God. For them, it was impossible to escape the divine call which made them speak on behalf of the defenseless, those whose rights had been violated, those who were victims of greed and power. This does not mean that no Christian should spend a portion, or even the better part, of his or her life in an ashram or a monastic enclosure; but it does mean that we cannot insert Jesus there. For Jesus, contemplation arose in the heart of the everyday world. Although he prayed, no mention is made of meditative "techniques" (or the deconstructing of techniques). He provided no steps for improving one's prayer life, nor did he create riddles to be pondered. The parables were neither inscrutable sayings nor indecipherable koans. For Jesus, apparently, prayer came naturally. He prayed because he had been taught to; he had inherited the piety of his parents and the faith of his religious tradition. He prayed because God was immediately real and present. He prayed, because what he saw around him drew prayer from his lips as spontaneously as children cry out to their parents. He prayed, above all, because his people suffered and were heavily burdened by hunger, taxes, political oppression, and maybe from disappointment: a people who boasted so much of the power of their God had very little to show for their privileged status. In short, the contemplative life of Jesus was formed in a context of social and political struggle.

Christian spirituality in this age of transition is going to take one of its bearings from a new form of prayer. I do not mean a new prayer or meditation technique, such as centering prayer or "Christian Zen" exercises. It does not have to do with devotions, such as the rosary, or the devout reading of scripture, or the Stations of the Cross. Rather, the form of prayer has to do with what informs and shapes the way we pray and relate to God. We shall learn this, furthermore, not from books or courses on spirituality, but from the poor themselves. But they will teach us, not because they have any special insight into prayer or the divine mystery; they seldom do. Their faith, if they have any faith at all, tends to be extremely simple. They will teach by drawing us into the worlds of their neighborhoods and families, and into their experience of clutching onto survival.

In her moving account of prisoners awaiting execution, Helen Prejean does not say much explicitly about the effect these men had on her prayer; but she does tell us this:

> I am reading people like Gandhi, Alice Walker, Albert Camus, Dorothy Day, and Martin Luther King, and even the way I pray is changing. Before, I had asked God to right the wrongs and comfort the suffering. Now I know—I really know—that God entrusts those tasks to us.[16]

The men she writes about were hardly pious; they had nothing to teach her about prayer. Yet the situation in which she found herself became every bit as contemplative as an Indian ashram or a monastery in Kentucky. She made it contemplative by relating to the world of men on death row in a mode of faith. That world drew something new from her. Before, she prayed as an observer: moved by such human desperation and brokenness, she beheld the prison world from outside. Once inside the world of those men, however, her interior landscape became reconfigured: "Now I know—I really know—that God entrusts those tasks to us." God walks alongside of us, animating our imaginations and emboldening our hearts, so that together with God we might remake our society. God, she had learned, places the responsibility to do something about human misery and poverty in our hands. Clearly, she already knew that God was among the poor; otherwise, she would not have made the option to live and work among them. What she had not realized in the beginning was that the Christian contemplative must learn how to pray with her hands: "God entrusts those tasks to us."

A good thirty years later, when I was conducting a writers' workshop, a participant startled me by asking how I pray, and I blurted, "I don't. At least, I don't think I do. At least, if I do, I don't do it right." And at that instant I knew that the reason I don't think I pray (outside of repeating something like the Our Father, that is, which is sometimes praying and sometimes not) is that at some level, often beneath my awareness, I never stop muttering to God. I still don't think I'm doing it right, though. Shouldn't prayer be describable as something loftier than a background rumble?

Who one believes God to be is most accurately revealed not in any credo but in the way one speaks to God when no one else is listening.

—Nancy Mairs
from *Ordinary Time*

Conclusion

1. Is Our Faith Built on an Error?

As I was writing these pages, one question kept creeping up on me. Has Christianity been founded upon a two-thousand-year-old mistake? This question almost sounds absurd, and even raising it may be bordering on arrogance. What makes me (or any one of us) think that we would have reached a level of understanding unsurpassed by any of our forebears from which to render such a judgment?

Yet surely the question is not new. Over the centuries there have been numerous Christians who have abandoned their ancestral faith, and some of them did so out of the conviction that Christianity was not the "true" religion after all. Perhaps they merely resented its triumphalist claims. Perhaps they were offended by the contradiction which appears now and then between what Christians claim and what they do. Or perhaps they really did achieve some insight into the nature of things religious and perceived a structural inadequacy within the institution of Christianity itself.

At the turn of the century, the French theologian Alfred Loisy observed: "Jesus foretold the kingdom, and it was the Church that came."[1] His observation turned into an aphorism, and was taken in a direction he did not intend. (In fact, the form in which I had remembered it was "Jesus preached the kingdom of God and the church preached Jesus.") Loisy had attempted to respond to the work of the German church historian Adolf Harnack, whose study of the early church had led him to identify a marked discontinuity between Jesus' simple proclamation of the kingdom of God and the church's "hellenization" of Christian faith in terms of dogmas about Christ as the gospel took root in the wider non-Jewish world. To understand the dogmas one practically needed to be a philosopher.

Perhaps it was the recognition of such discontinuity which prompted Harnack to set about trying to discover the "essence" of Christianity, the "kernel within the husk," or the "gospel within the gospel." Something in Christian faith had to be able to translate from one cultural context to another, and he attempted to formulate what it was. On the surface, this makes sense: of course there has to be a transcultural dimension to the gospel which allows the church to proclaim the same message in different times and places, within different languages and cultures! This essence or core of faith has to be what provides the continuity between Jesus and the later ages of the church. Without some threads of continuity, the conclusion that the Christian religion rested on a mistake would be unavoidable.

The fact is that the study of the Bible and its history has brought to light a great number of loose ends in our understanding of the church and Jesus. As New Testament scholars have dug further into the gospel texts, and as books and articles on Jesus have multiplied, our unsureness about Jesus has only increased. There are not many things which can be stated definitively about him, apart from some bare historical information. The effort to pin down what exactly Jesus did or said is not unlike running into the uncertainty principle in modern physics; what is seen is simultaneously being distorted by the perspective of the viewer. Yet one realization has emerged. Some of the claims made by the church both about itself and about Jesus have not been able to withstand historical criticism. The statement that Jesus did not "found" the church, or that he did not intend to set up a new religion, illustrate the effect of such criticism. Neither did he intend to establish the sacramental system, or institute a separate priestly class among his followers. And he did not claim to be God.

All of this needs to be digested. Nothing is accomplished by a flight into traditionalism; the failure to face questions and conclusions openly and fearlessly leads to imprisoning the mind. Since Vatican II, the church has at least started to digest part of the enormous changes which modern biblical and historical scholarship have generated in our understanding of Christian origins. Yet every so often people start to choke, or protest that they have been given too much at once. In this case, we need to take time to get our bearings: to think, to pray, to listen to one another. At the same time, we need to beware both of becoming reflexively defensive against everything that sounds new, and of surrendering to the nihilism and despair which perpetually seek to engulf the aspirations and hopes of the human race. Perhaps this is what the letter to the Ephesians had in mind when it spoke of the powers of this present age:

> For our struggle is not against enemies of blood and flesh, but against the rulers, against the authorities, against the cosmic powers of this present darkness, against the spiritual forces of evil in the heavenly places (Eph 6:12).

But to return to our question: Does Christianity rest upon an ancient mistake? I sincerely believe the answer is no, but I also think the question does not accurately reflect what the problem is.

The development of a religion does not take place according to a recipe. If a recipe calls for baking powder, and I add baking soda to the batter, that is a mistake. I once did that, and had to throw away the whole batch of biscuits when my mother began gagging on one. But the unfolding of a religion is governed by the interplay of all sorts of factors—cultural, anthropological, sociological, economic, political, philosophical—which are clearly outside the purview and the control of the spiritual charism which marked its genesis. One can insist that Christianity has been guided by the Holy Spirit, but I believe that, to be fair, one has to be willing to extend the same claim to many other things in human history. After all, even though the people of Israel could scarcely have comprehended this, their God was just as concerned about the salvation of the poor of Egypt and Babylon as God was about the poor slaves of Israel. No one people or race, and no one faith tradition, can lay exclusive claim to possessing the Spirit.

The fact that the living God has "spoken" to us (as we say) through the scriptures of the Judeo-Christian tradition does not mean that the divine voice has not appeared among Hindus and Buddhists, or within the spiritual traditions of indigenous peoples everywhere. It does no good to argue that religious traditions apart from our own have been compromised by pagan practices, such as the barbarity of human sacrifice; for Christianity has to own the murderous intolerance of the Inquisition, while the Israelites' battle practice of utterly eliminating their defeated enemies who had been "devoted to destruction" cannot be laid at God's door. Both the Israelites and the inquisitors believed that they were acting according to God's will: Joshua had succeeded Moses as the divinely-appointed leader, and Innocent IV, who authorized the Inquisition to use torture, was a successor of Peter.

In short, the category of mistake does not really apply here, unless it is the mistake of supposing that there actually is some mysterious gospel essence which can pass from one cultural setting to another. Even the "spiritual" response of one critic to Harnack's work missed the point:

> On this account the Christianity which we have and should practise can only consist in the grateful acceptance of the reconciliation, the forgiveness of our sins in the blood of Christ, and in the life, struggle, and work, the loving, ministering, and suffering, the hoping and waiting in the power of His grace. This and nothing else can and shall be the Christianity for all times.[2]

What we possess is a story which can be narrated over and over, not an abstract, timeless essence which can be reduced to a series of doctrinal statements. It is this story which makes us distinctive, and not truths about the goodness and love of God, or about divine compassion and mercy, or about the forgiveness of enemies, or about sharing our bread with the hungry. All of these features derive from Israel's faith, which Jesus had inherited. But through his story—through his life, death and resurrection—this faith became the inheritance of the whole human race.

One can say, of course, that Christians have frequently lost touch with the spirit of Jesus, that is, with the charism of the gospel; sometimes even scandalously so, as anyone who knows the history of the papacy or the colonization of the New World would be aware. But the religious tradition was not dead. The great reform movements which developed around figures like Francis of Assisi or Ignatius Loyola, or the theological brilliance of an Edward Schillebeeckx or Karl Rahner in our own day, testify to the fact that God has not abandoned the church; the spirit of prophecy is still alive. A religion can lose sight of its original grace and spirit, and thus must regularly renew itself; but historical process and development do not obey a recipe.

Perhaps the heart of the problem, in a time of transition as well as in a time of renewal, is locating the original grace or the spirit of Jesus. To be sure, Christianity elevated Jesus to divine status and universalized his significance. It translated salvation from liberation of the poor and oppressed in this world to deliverance from the power of sin and the attainment of everlasting life. Many forces and conditions contributed to the rapid expansion of Christianity from its status as a sect within Judaism to its becoming the dominant western religion, and most of these were probably not religious. Yet these social and political influences pushed the "idea" of Christianity forward. Central to everything was the fact, as we have remarked often in these pages, that the God of Israel had become the God of the nations. Through the life, death and resurrection of Jesus Israel's God was revealed to be God-for-all-people.

However, there is a further detail that must be added. The God of Israel was also and preeminently the God of the poor. In fact, I would urge that, as a result of the story of Jesus and his people, the very notion of God is forever inseparable from the story of humanity's degrading squalor and enslavement, its hunger and its desperate cries for justice. When Christian faith "universalized," it carried with it the God of Jesus as the God for all people; *but it did not universalize Israel's historical experience as the experience of an oppressed people.* As a result, its vision of God's concern for the human race would remain blurred. That is not to say that the church was not concerned about the poor. One has only to peruse some of the burning sermons of the early bishops and writers to realize how much the church saw itself as charged with their defense.[3]

The blur arose as a result of forgetting the historical experience of Israel, and of Jesus, as the background of Jesus' story. The early Christians were not about to advocate a large-scale protest movement against the structural abuses, the injustice and the oppression which existed in the imperial world. That world was simply accepted; it was the way things were, and following God's will meant conforming oneself to that world, even to obeying its rulers and paying taxes, as Paul wrote to the Christians in Rome (Rom 13:1–7). Christians were looking for acceptance; they hardly wanted to be accused of disturbing the peace or being the emperor's enemies, although there were pockets of Christians who did not hesitate to identify Caesar and Rome in terms of diabolic opposition to the reign of God. The book of Revelation testifies to this. The gospel writers tended to let the Romans off the hook for the death of Jesus, and shifted the blame to the Jewish leaders. Yet clearly it was the Romans who put Jesus to death. Crucifixion was their penalty. Their procurator had rendered the death sentence. Their soldiers had done the torturing. Their taxes had impoverished the people. And whatever measure of tolerance they seemed to grant the Jews was violently and abruptly ended with the destruction of Jerusalem in the year 70.

The Christians, then, wanted peace. Besides, it would be hard to conceive that the Gentile converts, many of whom probably enjoyed Roman citizenship, would be prepared to engage in wholesale reform of social structures, or to preach a faith doing justice, or to make the preferential option for the poor the major theme of their preaching and evangelizing. And yet the story of Jesus does not take on its richest meaning until the record of suffering and hunger, of oppression and poverty, are remembered. That is why the theological contribution of the Latin American church in this period of postconciliar renewal has been so invaluable. It represents one of the key moments in the church's history which bear witness to God's abiding fidelity to the world and to the community of faith; for if God had abandoned the church, the prophetic voices in Latin America would never have arisen. We are recovering an important dimension of the gospel story. We are also finally universalizing Israel's historical experience, because in that we have discovered the voices of oppressed minorities everywhere. In terms of that experience, concern for the poor goes beyond merely being one of the things naturally expected of Jesus' followers. The whole experience of God that lies behind the story of Jesus remains unintelligible until God is seen to be God-for-the-poor:

> "The Spirit of the Lord is upon me,
>   because he has anointed me
>   to bring good news to the poor.

He has sent me to proclaim release to the captives
    and recovery of sight to the blind,
        to let the oppressed go free,
    to proclaim the year of the Lord's favor" (Lk 4:18–19).

This may explain why efforts to locate the "essence" of Christian faith, or to uncover its "transcultural moment" have been fruitless. Historical experience is neither timeless nor an essence; it is particular and concrete.

2. The Questions This Raises

Where does all this leave Christian spirituality today, in this moment of transition? Do spirituality and asceticism disappear in favor of a social and political program on behalf of the poor and victims of injustice? Is not the emphasis upon alleviating human misery simply the late twentieth-century equivalent of the nineteenth-century "social gospel" in which Jesus is presented as a teacher of "higher" ethical values and a reformer of society?

Once again, such questions have been biting at me as I have tried to think my way through some of my own experience as a Christian living in the northern hemisphere, perhaps privileged beyond the wildest dreams of the elites of the past. Yet, both vicariously and directly, I have found myself being pulled into a different world. While this experience would pale in comparison with those who have fully immersed themselves in the world of the poor, I believe I can at least follow the insight of those who have worked through their experience and wrestled with these very questions.

Yes, there is clearly a social component to the gospel message. One recalls the instruction of John the Baptist to those who approached him looking for guidance:

And the crowds asked him, "What then should we do?" In reply he said to them, "Whoever has two coats must share with anyone who has none; and whoever has food must do likewise" (Lk 3:10–11).

Yet this is not all that the gospel is concerned with. The gospel is also concerned with the transformation of human hearts and minds which is called conversion. But how does conversion happen? Does a person simply, by an act of the will, decide that he or she will "convert," or does something have to trigger this process? Conversion can certainly occur as a result of the word or message one has heard: the preaching of John the Baptist brought about the change of heart which led the crowds to ask, "What then should we do?" The fact that John answers this question by directing their attention to those who are even poorer than they are cannot be accidental. John could have answered any number of ways, but he reveals here that being mindful of the poor is the ultimate fruit of conversion. In the same way, Jesus answered the rich man, "Sell what you own, and give the money to the poor" (Mk 10:21). Once more, Jesus' directing the man's attention toward the poor (he might have suggested any number of pious causes) is hardly accidental. The change of heart which following Jesus would symbolize moves in the direction of becoming constantly mindful of those who have nothing.

We have traditionally associated transformation of mind and heart with an encounter with Jesus crucified, because the cross has been the symbol of our redemption. Yet if Jesus crucified is not simply the individual Jesus of Nazareth, or rather, if the crucified Jesus is a symbol of all the people of history crucified in humanity's bloody contest against injustice, then it is possible to see how contact with the poor can likewise bring about conversion. Those of us who have been privileged discover in that contact the real malice of sin and our own complicity in the evil that has dehumanized so many. Our redemption might very well consist in our letting ourselves be loved by God through the poor themselves. I do not mean that the poor will automatically love us, and that their love will be redemptive (that may or may not happen). Rather, I mean that God is already among them, and the God among them is the very God who loves us through the crucified Jesus.

3. What About Prayer?

What will happen to Christian prayer? I think the principal change may lie in the way we imagine ourselves whenever we place ourselves consciously in God's presence. Certainly, we will continue to voice our praise and thanksgiving, our sorrow and repentance, our needs and our hopes. At the same time, the Christian will never be able to forget God's question to Cain, "Where is your brother Abel?" (Gen 4:9) "Where is your brother, where is your sister?" This question will guide us each night as we examine our consciences, lest in any way we contribute to the abuse or exploitation of other men and women. But maybe even more importantly, such a question will keep our hearts directed toward others, because we never stand in God's presence alone. We always bring our sisters and brothers with us; and if we do not, then God surely does.

Christian prayer will continue to draw its grasp of the things of God from the story of Jesus. One has to know the story in order to explain to others what being in relation to God, as a Christian, means. There are many ways of relating to God, one through each of the world's great religions, and even perhaps through countless unwritten paths which individuals throughout history have chanced upon. Nevertheless, approaching God in the context of the story of Jesus represents something distinctive. And here, we have seen, what may be most characteristic of that story is that the God of Jesus is a God of and for the poor. The salvation of the rich and powerful depends upon their discovering the nature of this God, which they will be able to do only if they can crawl through the eye of a needle.

The dying and rising of Jesus are above all for the poor: Jesus died in solidarity with them, a victim of the same injustice which they endured and which ran contrary to the reign of God. To proclaim the reign of God was to protest the things which dehumanized people. In raising Jesus from the dead, God revealed unequivocally the divine "preferential option" to join the poor and the powerless in their historical struggle. The victory, ultimately, would be theirs. The salvation of the mighty and those of high estate would depend upon their recognizing the poor as their own brothers and sisters, and radically changing the way they live and act. For a person like Zacchaeus it meant immediately giving half of his possessions to the needy, and restoring fourfold whatever he had acquired unjustly. This has to be the greatest miracle story in the New Testament, the changing of a heart of stone into a heart of flesh.

For people today, the way to answering the gospel's challenge is more complex. It certainly calls for sharing what we have with those who are in need. But the way to do that, as the church has pointed out, requires a transformation of global economic and political structures so that the relations between nations, just like the relationships among individuals, are ever more informed by justice. No one person, no one community, no single nation can accomplish everything which needs to be done. The example of Zacchaeus is a model of individual asceticism. It consists of direct contact with the poor and sharing one's goods with them. Of course, in Zacchaeus' case justice required that he return what he had acquired through fraud; but he did so "fourfold."

There can be a corporate or national asceticism, too, which might express itself in terms of social programs and foreign aid. Some of this actually amounts to returning to third-world countries some of the wealth and resources of which they were robbed, either when they were colonies of European countries or at the mercy of multinational corporations. Sometimes the motivation for such giving is one of strategic self-interest: wealthy nations need to make grants and give assistance for the sake of domestic and international security. A society divided along lines of rich and poor becomes an unstable society; a world divided between rich and poor nations is an unstable world.

Yet even the gospel acknowledges that people will act in terms of their self-interest and make friends with the ones whom they may have cheated: "And I tell you, make friends for yourselves by means of dishonest wealth so that when it is gone, [the poor] may welcome you into the eternal homes" (Lk 16:9). The giving of foreign aid, and the supporting of social programs, may be likened to Luke's story about the dishonest manager who was commended for acting shrewdly.

For the Christians who pay taxes which support such programs, there is another way to view matters. Through foreign aid and through social programs, they are actually contributing something to alleviate the misery of the world. Through active involvement in the political process they can also make sure that their money really meets grave human needs. This, I would suggest, is a contemporary form of gospel asceticism. Eliminating the structures and conditions that create such misery, however, is another step and it requires a different level of conversion. Jesus addressed the call for repentance and conversion to individuals. Today his community makes the same address to "corporate persons," that is, to institutions and to nations.

4. Everything Centers on God

Yet at the center of all we have been saying lies the mystery of God. It is axiomatic for Christian spirituality that people find God in the measure that they see the world with compassion. There are two corollaries to this axiom. The first is that one finds God when one opens oneself to the world of the poor. The second is that the God of Christian faith is in a special way the God who is of and for the poor and the oppressed. Compassionate seeing is what reveals these truths: this, and the story of Jesus. Someone recently asked me, in all earnestness, "But why do you need to talk about God? Why not simply involve ourselves on behalf of the poor and work to transform social structures, to convert institutions and corporations? Why not be an atheist converted to justice? Is the idea of God necessary?"

I wish I had been able to respond to those questions with the abundance of detail and degree of reasonableness that this person was looking for. He had already read Michael Buckley's major study *At the Origins of Modern Atheism*, which traces the intellectual roots of unbelief today.[4] His problem was not theoretical, and if it had been, I would still not have been able to help. One immediately starts to think about the "anonymous believers" of Matthew 25, who serve Jesus without ever realizing that it was Jesus who was present in the person who was hungry, or without clothes, or a refugee, or in prison. One thinks about the innumerable men and women of good will who try to do what is right even though they never explicitly call upon God. One also wonders what the fate of God will be in a postmodern era, where people have found ways to describe experience adequately without recourse to the notion of God. Is it true that if the notion of God were to disappear from our vocabulary, we would turn into a race of monsters?

For me, there are two responses to the question about God, and both of them have been confirmed by experience. I recall once more the words of Rahner's Ignatius, for their boldness, their simplicity and their honesty: "God himself; I knew God himself, not simply human words describing him. I knew God and the freedom which is an integral part of him." The first response is an appeal to the story of Jesus. I believe that we live out of stories, not out of metaphysics, philosophies of life, or sophisticated forms of literary criticism. In the end, stories are all that we have, and therein lies a great clue about us. Harnack wrote: "It is not a question of a 'doctrine' being handed down by uniform repetition or arbitrarily distorted; it is a question of a *life*, again and again kindled afresh, and now burning with a flame of its own."[5] And Alan Jones has written:

> It is better to enter into the drama of God's love than to wait on the edge until every dogma is properly understood. Dogmas are like the love letters that lovers keep and look at from time to time to remind them of the story that binds them together.[6]

It is the gospel story that communicates life; indeed, the "drama of God's love" becomes the foundation of the way we look at ourselves and the world. And we allow it to do so because the story of Jesus is also a story about God. *That* is what makes it interesting.

The second response is that the experience of God is affirmed within the world of the poor. I am not sure that I shall ever be able to do full justice to this important insight, the way that the Peruvian writer Gustavo Gutierrez has done in *The God of Life*,[7] or the way that the Brazilian writer Leonardo Boff has done in *Passion of Christ, Passion of the World*.[8] This basic truth can only be confirmed through experience. Moreover, there is nothing private about this. Experience is certainly personal, or it may be corporate, as when many share the same experience. But the experience of God does not happen apart from a radical reorientation of heart, mind and soul toward the world of the poor. This change is not merely the result of a change of ideas. In other words, we cannot read ourselves into conversion to the poor (at least I could not); we need to encounter them.

This encounter cannot be just a matter of meeting people who happen to be trapped in poverty: a person could react to that with fear and horror, and want only to flee. God surely cannot be *there*! This is what first happened to me when I stepped into the streets of Calcutta. Instead, the encounter has to be marked by grace. I know no other way to describe this. At some point, one must learn to look at the hardness of human misery with compassion. The moment one does so, everything changes. One sees there only brothers and sisters, suffering, or hungry, or uneducated, or chronically unemployed. One also sees them and their condition with hope: their lives could be different. And one also discovers a desperate surge of life within them, trying to break to the surface and enable them to survive. This is what is responsible for the creation of base communities in the Latin American church; it is also responsible for people resorting to stealing, or to revolution. The poor must eat today, and they must find a means obtaining food tomorrow, without fear.

Among the poor, one senses humanity's age-old thirst for justice and freedom. One understands for the first time why the God of Jesus is of and for the poor. God, one realizes, is there, among those people, locked as they are in cycles of poverty and hopelessness. They flee violence and hunger in the countryside, only to land in squalid slums and shantytowns sprawling from urban centers. And hunger and poverty are the lot of the majority of the earth's people. The realization that God dwells among them is neither glamorous nor romantic. Life among the poor remains just as hard as before. The poor, too, need to be converted. They, too, have to learn how to discover God in their midst, and to believe in the God whose one desire is to deliver them from their powerlessness, their want and their wounded dignity.

But for us, the ones trying to squeeze through the needle's eye, there comes the moment of grace. For them Jesus died, and for them, God raised him from the dead. I want to be with them because that is where Jesus is; that is where he has always been. That is where he is calling us. Strain as I might to visualize God, the only image that comes to mind is my brother's face, the only sound my sister's voice. And when I try to imagine what eternity with God might be like, all those faces come together in one enormous communion. The early community which bequeathed to us the first letter of John wanted us to understand how close, yet how profound is the mystery which binds us: "for those who do not love a brother or a sister whom they have seen, cannot love God whom they have not seen" (4:20). Even in glory, we may only behold the face of God through the faces of so many sisters and brothers: but what holds everything in that blessed vision together is love.

We learn how to love by loving what God loves. Perhaps that is what draws us toward the poor. And the great insight? That God loves us through them.

5. Prayer and Jesus

There is still one last question. Should we continue to address Jesus in prayer? I have two reasons for raising this question. The first is that there is a truly *human* experience of God, that is, an experience of God which does not depend upon any particular religious tradition for its occurrence. This absolutely has to be the case, if it is true that all of us come from God, all of us are of God (in that we have been formed in the divine image and likeness), and all of us are living toward God, whether we are conscious of this or not. The destiny of the human being is, we believe, union with God in a loving communion with *all* God's daughters and sons, whether they adhered to a given religious tradition or not.

Although the path to God through organized religion has been the ordinary way for most of us, religions and their institutions are only instrumental. God reveals or shares the divine mystery in and through religions, but not exclusively through them: through the things which happen in our world and the innumerable events of our lives, through decisions taken or not taken, through memories, through relationships good and bad with other men and women, through literature, art and music, in short, through many things which would not ordinarily be described as religious. If human salvation depended only upon the world's religions, then what would happen to those who for various reasons do not feel drawn to affiliate with one of them? And what would happen when the religious institutions themselves became encrusted over time and resistant to renewal, or destructively fundamentalist? No; human salvation is too important for the divine self-giving to be restricted to the domain of organized religions.

While I believe that even people who do not belong to a religious tradition develop some way of relating to God (even though they might not describe their inner experience that way), the activity of praying is generally regarded as religious in the formal sense. Christian spiritual writers have talked about higher prayer forms—mystical states—which normally emerge through longstanding practice at prayer and meditation. Prayer by means of image and word gradually gives way to a wordless silence in the presence of God. In that presence, even the word "God" can be stripped of all meaning: one is simply "there," in the presence of mystery which grasps mind and heart, empties them, yet in a strange way also fills them. One is totally taken over by love. And why call this love? Because that is the experience: the experience of being overwhelmed by love; one knows the experience when one has had it.

Being with God, silently, is not some mind trick for achieving inner peace. In fact, such wordless prayer is generally preceded by a great deal of interior wrestling as we get to know ourselves better (which encompasses all the attitudes, memories and experiences, likes and dislikes, and so forth, that make us who we are) and as we gain insight into the self-destructive nature of sin. Reaching enlightenment requires purification of soul, and this happens to Christians and non-Christians alike who devote themselves to searching for God.

While considerably more could be said about this, I want only to say that this "higher state" is in no way inconsistent with prayer through imagination. In fact, to think of this state as "higher" probably renders it a disservice; it might be like arguing over the merits of different kinds of music. Besides, after hearing someone speak about "high" mystical stages of prayer, ordinary people might feel themselves left out; or else they might want to master the technique for grasping or seizing the so-called "higher" states, which is the surest way never to reach one. There is absolutely nothing wrong with being immersed in the story of Jesus, where our feelings and imaginations are continually being aroused and nurtured by the scenes and encounters, the sayings and events of the gospels.

The fact is that we do grow or advance in prayer the longer we remain faithful to its practice. Prayer is essentially a way of relating to the mystery of God, and just as our relationships develop as people remain faithful to one another, so too does the human relationship with God, whether or not "God" is explicitly called on by name. God finds ways of entering human lives that go beyond whatever we can conceive of. And "God" can disappear altogether, as a person lives ever more steadily in a state of loving and being loved. Within such a state, sometimes it does not even feel right to address God, in the way one person would speak to another, because the mystery of God has become so all-pervading:

> Even before a word is on my tongue,
>   O Lord, you know it completely.
> You hem me in, behind and before,
>   and lay your hand upon me (Ps 139:4–5).

Awkwardness gives way to silence, as the mind gives up groping for words. The experience of being so fully known leaves the human spirit speechless.

Nevertheless, we should not be worried that remaining immersed in the story of Jesus represents a "lower" stage of prayer, or a somewhat less mature way of relating to God than the purified prayer states of the mystics. As we saw earlier, Jesus was not a mystic, either. If the higher contemplative states require both practice and time, then Jesus probably did not live long enough to reach these levels of meditation. Besides, the pursuit of spiritual development does not appear to have been part of his mission. A person can grow *in the story* and discover the God of Jesus there. There is no need to feel compelled to abandon the story, with the particularity and concreteness of its images, faces and voices, in favor of something universal and transcendent. The gospel story can work us over and purify our souls, turning us into men and women who continually pray and live as people who walk in the company of Jesus. Living in the story can turn ordinary people into mystics whose entire orientation is being-for-others.

I said that there were two reasons for raising the question about whether we should continue to address Jesus in prayer. The second reason I would offer goes back to a reflection we made earlier.

All prayer is directed to God, even when we imagine ourselves addressing Mary, or one of the other saints, or even Jesus. If we were to analyze those inner conversations, I believe we would discover that we have, in effect, been telling God something, but at the same time either we needed to put a face on God, or we did not feel worthy of approaching God directly. In either case, God sees through the subtleties of our logic and meets us where we are. The face may look like that of a saint, but the presence behind the image is truly God's. We may sense ourselves unworthy to stand in God's presence alone, but this does not change the nature of things. God is there, whether we think of God being there directly, or not. God absolutely hears the prayer which speaks of our unworthiness, without any mediation on the part of one of God's holy ones.

The whole notion of mediation is perhaps something of an artifice. Nor does it make sense to try to give this artifice some theological justification by arguing that God willed things this way. It is not as if God, knowing that we would feel the need of mediators and intercessors, decreed that the saints would fill this role for our benefit. I believe we are simply talking about how human beings manage their feelings of unworthiness, sinfulness and inadequacy in the presence of God. There is nothing harmful about this, so long as one does not dismiss out of hand those who insist that they do not feel any need for mediators or intercessors. One who does not experience such a need may well have achieved a great deal of familiarity with God.

Needless to say, the notion of mediation does appear in scripture. For example, after urging its readers to adopt the practice of praying "for everyone," and especially for those in positions of authority, the first letter to Timothy states:

> This [practice] is right and acceptable in the sight of God our Savior, who desires everyone to be saved and to come to the knowledge of the truth. For
>
> > there is one God;
> > there is also one mediator
> > between God and humankind,
> > Christ Jesus, himself human . . . (1 Tim 2:3–5).

Yet the emphasis here seems to fall on the *oneness* of God, God's being the "savior" who wills the salvation of all human beings, and the *humanness* of Jesus. Whatever distance humanity may have experienced between itself and its creator has been canceled out. In other words, in looking for God, we never need to fear that we are gazing into a nameless, faceless silence. God can be addressed in and through one of us, namely, "Christ Jesus, himself human." And the believer who prays on behalf of others (particularly "for kings and all who are in high positions"), that is, who acts as a "mediator" for his or her neighbor, ought not to think that such a prayer is going to induce God to become more merciful. God already desires the salvation of all. Rather, such a prayer brings about a change in those who make it, rendering them more compassionate and rendering them more like Christ Jesus. For each of us in our own way helps others to discover the face and voice of God.

Again, the letter to the Hebrews does speak of Jesus in the role of mediator:

> For we do not have a high priest who is unable to sympathize with our weaknesses, but we have one who in every respect has been tested as we are, yet without sin. . . . Consequently, he is able for all time to save those who approach God through him, since he always lives to make intercession for them. (Heb 4:15, 7:25).

There are several observations to make here, however. One of the reasons for the letter's insistence upon the once-for-all character of Jesus' "priesthood" is its theological position that the old dispensation has been abrogated. The Temple, with its priesthood and sacrificial cult, has been replaced by something new. In other words, the theological stress falls more heavily on Jesus as replacing the old than on a reaffirmation of the concepts of priesthood, sacrifice, mediation and intercession. It might even be argued that the letter has, whether intentionally or not, "deconstructed" those concepts, with Jesus replacing the religious and liturgical institutions of Israel.

Even though the church eventually adopted the symbolism of cult, priesthood and sacrifice, the church cannot appeal to the letter to the Hebrews as justification for doing so.[9] But it is also possible to move outside those cultic categories altogether and explain the significance of Jesus for us in other terms. In fact, this is exactly what we do when we say that the story of Jesus has become a story of God. Story, not cult, provides the proper categories for talking about Jesus today.

The words of Stephen, "Lord Jesus, receive my spirit" (Acts 7:59), certainly evidence the fact that the early Christians adopted the habit of addressing Jesus in prayer. Let me also admit at this point that I do talk with Jesus. He has a personal presence in my thinking and acting, my imagining and deciding, the theological basis of which is the resurrection. I take that part of the story with the utmost literalness: God raised Jesus from the dead, and God did so in order that Jesus might abide among us and give God that face and voice which we need and seek. Through the resurrection, Jesus is definitively one with the Father, just as all of us hope to be.

But the resurrection does not stand by itself, apart from the rest of the story and all that Jesus did and said while he walked among us—the one from Nazareth "who was a prophet mighty in deed and word before God and all the people" (Lk 24:19). The resurrection not only forms a piece with the rest of the story; it is the rest of the story which tells us how to interpret what Jesus' being raised from the dead was all about. As a result, we can speak to Jesus in any of the gospel scenes because throughout those scenes moves the presence of Jesus risen.

Many children are known to carry on conversations with imaginary friends, but apparently they also realize that these companions are "make-believe." It relieved me to learn that this is both normal and healthy, since I can remember engaging in this sort of fantasy myself. I believed that guardian angels were real and could honestly be talked to. But children also outgrow this need.

Grown men and women may carry on brief conversations with a deceased husband or wife, parent or grandparent, or a much loved friend, much in the way that Tevye in the musical *Fiddler on the Roof* charmed us with his ongoing conversation with God. Often people sincerely believe that the deceased person is now alive somewhere else and not only can be addressed, but remains interested in the affairs of the living. Often, too, their words conceal the fact that someone is actually speaking to God, for the deceased would not be "alive" to us at all unless we believed that they now enjoy definitive oneness with the Father.

Carrying on a conversation with Jesus, however, is very different. Jesus was not someone whom we personally knew, like a parent or a spouse; we cannot insert him into the familiar surroundings with which we associate our loved ones who have died: in the usual chair, in the garden or in the garage, in a particular home. Each time we eat a certain food, we cannot say, "Jesus always liked this" or "Jesus used to insist that we have this once a week." In short, Jesus does not fit into our worlds that way. Even if we succeeded in reconstructing his world through historical imagination, we would not belong there, any more than Jesus could step comfortably into ours.

Then why try to talk with him? Why not simply recognize the story for what it is, and approach God directly? We may want to hold onto the story, because it provides the metaphors and symbols through which we interpret the world and order our lives. But do we need to hold on to Jesus?

The fundamental reason is that we live in and from the gospel story, because the whole story, from beginning to end, is not just about Jesus, nor about Jesus and his contemporaries. The story is not even just about us, or about the poor and the oppressed of the earth. The gospel story is essentially a story about God. To say that we experience God through history and through a story, through the lives of other men and women, and especially through the poor, is to speak about a particular way of knowing and experiencing God. All of this is what makes the Christian faith distinctive, and it is what makes those who follow this faith into a distinctive kind of human being. The prophetic heart which hears the anguish of the poor and their cries for justice has shared God's own concern for the defenseless, the imprisoned, those cheated out of their of land or out of their wages. This marks a particular kind of human being. The compassionate heart which recognizes all men and women as belonging to itself, and which at the same time throws itself into making the world ever more human and ever more just, whatever the cost, represents a particular kind of human being. Whose image and likeness do people like this bear, if not the image and likeness of the God of Jesus?

I speak to Jesus as I would speak to God, not because Jesus and God are identical, but because I do not know how to address the awesome silence of the divine mystery. I speak to Jesus as I would to

God because I believe that God's true home lies on earth, among us, so long as the human race continues to exist, where Jesus lived for a while among us. I speak to Jesus as I would to God, and not to a deceased relative, because it is Jesus' concerns that I have made my own, and I have done so because I cannot imagine God having any other concerns except these. I speak to Jesus as I would to God because I believe that Jesus is in God, and God in Jesus, in a way that I hope will one day be true for all of us.

While I do not believe that Jesus is God pure and simple, without any qualification, I have not been able to picture God apart from Jesus, either. Yet the conviction lying behind all of this, apart from which what I have just said would make no sense, is based in the way I have come to hear the story. The point is not so much that Jesus lives, a person eternally detached from time and place so that he might be universally available; the point is that the story lives, and he lives within it. Or to take things one step higher, the point is not that God lives, dwelling in some place apart, from which God sends messengers into the world, or pious inspirations; but that the story lives, from creation to resurrection, and that God lives within it. Do away with the stories, and God will cease to exist. Not just the God of Israel, or the God of Jesus, but the holy mystery itself.

Story is the product of imagination, and we are nothing, if not creatures who have the power to imagine. To think, yes, and to will: but above all, the power to create new worlds and re-create old ones. With imagination there goes memory, and with memory comes tradition. With imagination there are dreams, and with dreaming comes the future. I speak to Jesus because I live in his story. My entire existence speaks to God when that story lives in me.

Notes

Preface

1. The book was published by The University of Chicago Press (1984), and the review appeared in *The Heythorp Journal* 39:3 (1988), 395–97.

2. Robert Bolt, *A Man for All Seasons* (New York: Vintage Books, 1960), p. 38.

3. *Holy the Firm* (San Francisco: Harper & Row, 1977), pp. 61–62.

Introduction

1. An intriguing New Age work is *A Course in Miracles* (Glen Ellen, Ca.: Foundation for Inner Peace, 2nd ed. revised [3 volumes], 1976). Marilyn Ferguson's *The Aquarian Conspiracy* (New York: The Putnam Publishing Group, 1980), which is far more benign than the title suggests, represents New Age thinking very well. A helpful set of articles evaluating New Age spirituality can be found in the July 1993 issue of *The Way*. One of the articles suggests that New Age spirituality may have peaked.

2. Boston: Beacon Press, 1993.

3. For example, *Teaching a Stone to Talk* (San Francisco: Harper & Row, 1982), *Holy the Firm* (San Francisco: Harper & Row, 1977), and, although not explicitly religious but certainly meditative, *Pilgrim at Tinker Creek* (New York: Harper & Row, 1974).

4. New York: Farrar, Straus & Giroux, 1992.

5. Books do not have to be ostensibly "spiritual" to qualify as spiritual reading, however. Wherever the human spirit is engaged, nourished, or challenged, there we have contributions to humanity's spiritual literature. And if that literature leads to a more profound understanding of our common humanity, if it leads us to weep over the jealousy, ambition and greed which kills the human soul, or if it helps us to grasp the message and mission of the gospel with fresh insight, then it would not be off the mark even to call such writing religious. One Jesuit friend regularly returns to Tolstoy's *War and Peace* for precisely this reason. I would turn to a work such as Nancy Scheper-Hughes' *Death Without Weeping: The Violence of Everyday Life in Brazil* (Berkeley: University of California Press, 1993). Dorothy Day wrote: "Both Dostoevski and Tolstoi made me cling to a faith in God." And referring to Dostoevski, she said, "[N]ow I read him with an understanding of men and suffering" (*The Long Loneliness* [New York: Harper & Row, 1952], pp. 43, 107).

6. For example, *Clinging: The Experience of Prayer* (San Francisco: Harper & Row, 1984).

7. For example, *Awake in the Spirit: A Practical Handbook on Prayer* (New York: Crossroad, 1992), and *Centering Prayer* (New York: Doubleday, 1980).

8. Nouwen's writing on the spirituality of ministry is fairly well known. But see his *Life of the Beloved: Spiritual Living in a Secular World* (New York: Crossroad, 1992).

9. For example, *Paying Attention to God* (Notre Dame: Ave Maria Press, 1990), *Now Choose Life* (Mahwah, N.J.: Paulist Press, 1990), and *A Hunger for God* (Paulist Press, 1991).

10. New York: HarperCollins, 1992. Moore writes as a psychotherapist, and occasionally in the book he speaks of his Catholic background. Yet throughout an entire book on the "care of the soul," the mystery of God never figures in. He writes: "We care for the soul by honoring its expressions, by giving it time and opportunity to reveal itself, and by living life in a way that fosters the depth, interiority, and quality in which it flourishes. Soul is its own purpose and end" (p. 304).

11. New York: HarperCollins, 1992. Leech writes: "If we are to rescue Christian spirituality from its captivity to individualism and the culture of false inwardness, we will need to recover the sense of its

social character, indeed, the sense of the social character of the gospel itself" (p. 17).

12. See, for instance, Leonardo Boff, *When Theology Listens to the Poor* (San Francisco: Harper & Row, 1988), and Gustavo Gutierrez, "Theology from the Experience of the Poor," in the *Proceedings* of the 47th convention of the Catholic Theological Society of America (June 1992), pp. 26–33. Also, Monika Hellwig, *Whose Experience Counts in Theological Reflection?* (Milwaukee: Marquette University Press, 1982).

13. Maryknoll, N.Y.: Orbis Books, 1984.

14. Maryknoll, N.Y.: Orbis Books, 1976. Running in a similar vein is the work of Carlos Mesters, writing from his experience in Brazil.

15. For example, see William Connolly and William Barry, *The Practice of Spiritual Direction* (New York: Seabury Press, 1982), and Kenneth Leech, *Soul Friend: The Practice of Christian Spirituality* (San Francisco: Harper & Row, 1980).

16. See Matthew Fox, *Creation Spirituality: Liberating Gifts for the Peoples of the Earth* (New York: HarperCollins, 1991).

17. One way of calling to mind many of the issues, problems and developments which have occurred would be to look through the collection of Richard McBrien's columns spanning the years since the council which appear in his *Report on the Church: Catholicism After Vatican II* (New York: HarperCollins, 1992).

18. As a good introduction to the Jesus story, I encourage my students to read Albert Nolan, *Jesus Before Christianity* (Maryknoll, N.Y.: Orbis Books, 1976, 1992). I should also like to suggest my own *Talking About Jesus Today* (Paulist Press, 1993).

19. Bede Griffiths, *The Marriage of East and West* (Springfield, Ill.: Templegate Publishers, 1982), pp. 148–49. Bede Griffiths was a Benedictine monk who spent almost forty years of his monastic life in India, where he died in May, 1993.

Part One: Where Shall We Look for God?

1. Karl Rahner, *Foundations of Christian Faith*, trans. William Dych (New York: Seabury Press, 1978), p. 49.

2. *Dreams of a Final Theory: The Search for the Fundamental Laws of Nature* (New York: Pantheon Books, 1992), pp. 256, 257.

3. I am thinking, for example, of those scientists whose views appear in *Cosmos, Bios, Theos*, ed. Henry Margeneau and Roy Abraham Varghese (LaSalle, Ill.: Open Court Publishing Co., 1992). See also Arthur Peacocke, *Theology for a Scientific Age* (Oxford: Basil Blackwell, 1990); John Polkinghorne, *Science and Providence* (Boston: Shambhala Publications, 1989); Ian Barbour, *Religion in an Age of Science* (San Francisco: Harper & Row, 1990); and Paul Davies, *God and the New Physics* (New York: Simon & Schuster, 1983).

4. Kenneth Leech, *Experiencing God: Theology as Spirituality* (San Francisco: Harper & Row, 1985), p. 8.

5. "Ignatius of Loyola Speaks to a Modern Jesuit" in *Ignatius Loyola* (with Paul Imhoff [New York: Collins, 1979]), p. 12.

6. Saint Augustine, *Confessions*, Book I:4, trans. Henry Chadwick (New York: Oxford University Press, 1991), pp.4–5.

7. *God For Us: The Trinity and Christian Life* (San Francisco: HarperCollins, 1991), pp. 382–83.

8. *Conjectures of a Guilty Bystander* (Garden City, New York: Doubleday & Co., 1966), p. 140.

9. St. Thomas Aquinas, *Summa Theologiae: A Concise Translation*, ed. Timothy McDermott (Westminster, Maryland: Christian Classics, 1989), p. 31.

10. Mark C. Taylor, *Nots* (Chicago: University of Chicago Press, 1993), pp. 26–27.

11. From the *Cloud of Unknowing* in Harvey Egan, S.J., *An Anthology of Christian Mysticism* (Collegeville: The Liturgical Press, 1991), pp. 368–69.

12. "God Is Far From Us" in *The Content of Faith: The Best of Karl Rahner's Theological Writings*, ed. Karl Lehmann, Albert Raffelt, and Harvey Egan (New York: Crossroad Publishing Co., 1992), pp. 216–17.

Part Two: Where Shall We Look for Jesus?

1. Samuel G. Freedman, *Upon This Rock: The Miracles of a Black Church* (New York: HarperCollins, 1993), p. 132.

2. This calls for a qualification. Each one of us, whether in small ways or large ones, contributes to the climate of sin in the world. Our corporate sinfulness creates the conditions which lead to evil and injustice. From this perspective, it can be said that not only are we responsible for the death of Jesus; we are likewise responsible (in large or small ways) for the unjust deaths of each one of our brothers and sisters who falls victim to poverty, injustice, hunger or oppression. We share corporate responsibility and blame for the sinfulness which exists in our world.

Similarly, it can happen that a sudden encounter with any instance of such suffering will lead us to both an awareness of our own share of the blame and of our need for forgiveness. The dead victim cannot forgive us, but the living victims can. If that encounter ultimately leads us to a change of heart and also leads us to dedicate ourselves to working against the dehumanizing conditions in our world, then we will have experienced the grace of forgiveness. Moments like these are sacramental. To be sure, the cross can mediate an experience of God's forgiveness. But so, too, can every other instance of human suffering caused by the world's sinfulness.

3. A book which expands on this precision is John J. Collins, *Between Athens and Jerusalem* (New York: Crossroad Publishing Co., 1983). A very ample study can be found in Louis H. Feldman, *Jew and Gentile in the Ancient World* (Princeton: Princeton University Press, 1993). I am indebted to Frederick J. Murphy for referring me to the first title, and to Daniel J. Harrington, S.J., for referring me to the second.

4. *Decrees of the Ecumenical Councils*, ed. Norman P. Tanner, S.J. (Washington and London: Georgetown University Press and Sheed & Ward, 1990), volume 2:1069.

5. John R. Donahue explains: "Compassion is that quality which, when present in human beings, enables them to move from one world to the other: from the world of helper to the one needing help; from the world of the innocent to that of the sinner. Under Luke's tutelage the parable [of the Good Samaritan] becomes *a paradigm of the compassionate vision* which is the presupposition for ethical action." See *The Gospel in Parable* (Philadelphia: Fortress Press, 1988), p. 132.

6. The entry under *templum* in the *Dictionnaire Etymolgique de la Langue Latine* (Paris, 1959 [fourth edition]) quotes the Latin

author Varro: "contemplari dictum est a templo, i.e. loco qui ab omni parte aspici, uel ex quo omnis pars uideri potest, quem antiqui templum nominabant."

7. Readers may recall what Hans Küng wrote: "Jesus apparently cannot be fitted in anywhere: neither with the rulers nor with the rebels, neither with the moralizers nor with the silent ascetics. He turns out to be provocative, both to right and to left. Backed by no party, challenging on all sides: 'The man who fits no formula.' He is neither a philosopher nor a politician, neither a priest nor a social reformer. Is he a genius, a hero, a saint? Or a religious reformer? But is he not more radical than someone who tries to re-form, reshape things? Is he a prophet? But is a 'last' prophet, who cannot be surpassed, a prophet at all? . . . He is on a different plane: apparently closer than the priests to God, freer than the ascetics in regard to the world, more moral than the moralists, more revolutionary than the revolutionaries." From *On Being a Christian*, trans. Edward Quinn (Garden City, New York: Doubleday & Co., 1976), p. 212.

8. *The Partings of the Ways* (Philadelphia: Trinity Press International, 1991), pp. 258–59.

9. Dunn, *Partings of the Ways*, p. 182.

10. Adela Yarbro Collins, *The Beginning of the Gospel: Probings of Mark in Context* (Minneapolis: Fortress Press, 1992), p. 37.

11. James Dunn comments: "[W]here prophecy is active the community is compelled to think about its faith and life even more . . . This charisma is the guarantor of spiritual health and growth. Without it the community cannot exist as the body of Christ; it has been abandoned by God." See *Jesus and the Spirit* (Philadelphia: Westminster Press, 1975), p. 233.

12. I am using "classic" in the sense developed by David Tracy in *The Analogical Imagination* (New York: Crossroad Publishing Co., 1981). Two key features in the production of a text which has come to be regarded as classic are what he calls the intensification of experience and particularity. The human and religious experience which lies behind the very particular story of Israel and the story of Jesus speaks to us as we read and interpret those ancient texts. One reason why those stories continue to engage our imaginations is that they help us understand ourselves and those experiences of the world which are generally

termed "religious." They also have the power to move us in the direction of what the gospel refers to as conversion.

13. See Hans Küng, *Judaism*, trans. John Bowden (New York: Crossroad Publishing Co., 1992), pp. 315–18.

Part Three: Getting Our Bearings in a Time of Transition

1. William Temple (1881–1944), quoted in *The Oxford Dictionary of Quotations*. I discovered the remark in a review by Roy Shaw in the May 8, 1993 issue of *The Tablet* of the recently published fourth edition of this work.

2. The story of Cyrus can be found in the book of Ezra.

3. First-hand accounts of injustice have an almost scripture-like quality about them. See, for example, *Nunca Mas: The Report of the Argentine National Commission on the Disappeared* (New York: Farrar, Straus & Giroux, 1986); or Ricardo Falla, *Massacres in the Jungle: Ixcán, Guatemala, 1975–1982*, trans. Julia Howland (Boulder, Colorado: Westview Press, 1994) or portions of *Ignacio: The Diary of a Maya Indian of Guatemala*, translated and edited by James Sexton (Philadelphia: University of Pennsylvania Press, 1992). What links all such accounts is the cry for justice, which was the cry of the people for deliverance in the book of Exodus.

4. Paul Kennedy, *Preparing for the Twenty-First Century* ((New York: Random House, 1993), pp. 25–26, 46.

5. Quoted from a front-page article by James Brooke in *The New York Times* on Sunday, July 4, 1993.

6. See Penny Lernoux, *People of God: The Struggle for World Catholicism* (New York: Penguin Books, 1989), pp. 157–60.

7. "Ignatius Loyola: Trial or Project?" in *Signs of the Times: Theological Reflections*, ed. Alfred T. Hennelley, S.J. (Maryknoll, N.Y.: Orbis, Books, 1993), pp. 149–75.

8. In No. 42 of his encyclical letter *Populorum Progressio (On the Development of Peoples)* Paul VI referred to this wholeness as "complete" or "integral" humanism: "What must be aimed at is complete humanism. And what is that if not the fully-rounded development of the whole man and of all men?" See *The Gospel of Peace and*

Justice: Catholic Social Teaching since Pope John, presented by Joseph Gremillion (Maryknoll, N.Y.: Orbis Books, 1976), p. 400.

9. Two serious yet very helpful articles are: Patrick H. Byrne, "*Ressentiment* and the Preferential Option for the Poor" and Stephen J. Pope, "Proper and Improper Partiality and the Preferential Option for the Poor" in *Theological Studies* 54:2 (1993), 213–71.

10. This point is wonderfully developed by Sebastian Moore in his book *The Crucified Jesus Is No Stranger* (New York: Seabury Press, 1977). It has been recently republished by Paulist Press.

11. After examining the theme of meal-taking in Luke, Robert J. Karris concluded: "Jesus got himself crucified because of the way he ate." See *Luke: Artist and Theologian* (Mahwah, N.J.: Paulist Press, 1985), p. 70.

12. David N. Power, *The Eucharistic Mystery: Revitalizing the Tradition* (New York: Crossroad Publishing Co., 1992), pp. 347–48.

13. See, for example, Bede Griffiths, *The Marriage of East and West* (Templegate: Springfield, Ill., 1982) and *A New Vision of Reality* (Templegate, 1989).

14. Karl Rahner, "The Spirituality of Church of the Future" in *Theological Investigations*, volume 20 (New York: Crossroad Publishing Co., 1981), pp. 143–53.

15. See Adela Yarbro Collins, *The Beginning of the Gospel* (Minneapolis: Fortress Press, 1992), pp. 12 and 22, where she cites the work of Vernon Robbins *Jesus the Teacher* (Philadelphia: Fortress Press, 1984). Donald Senior provides a good description of the meaning of disciple in *Jesus: A Gospel Portrait* (Mahwah, New Jersey: Paulist Press, 1992), pp. 51–61.

16. From *Dead Man Walking: An Eyewitness Account of the Death Penalty in the United States* (New York: Random House, 1993), p. 11. Helen Prejean is a religious, a member of the Sisters of St. Joseph of Medaille.

Conclusion

1. Loisy clearly meant this in a positive sense, because he continued: "she [the Church] came, enlarging the form of the gospel, which

it was impossible to preserve as it was, as soon as the Passion closed the ministry of Jesus." See *The Gospel and the Church*, trans. Christopher Home (New York: Charles Scribner's Sons, 1904), p. 166.

2. Hermann Cremer, *A Reply to Harnack on the Essence of Christianity*, trans. Bernhard Pick (New York: Funk & Wagnalls, 1903), pp. 266–67.

3. For example, see the selections which appear in St. John Chrysostom, *On Wealth and Poverty*, trans. Catharine P. Roth (Crestwood, N.Y.: St. Vladimir's Seminary Press, 1984); and Charles Avila, *Ownership: Early Christian Teaching* (Maryknoll, N.Y.: Orbis Books, 1983).

4. New Haven: Yale University Press, 1990.

5. Adolf Harnack, *What is Christianity?*, trans. Thomas Saunders (New York: G. P. Putnam's Sons, 1901), p. 11.

6. Alan Jones, *Passion for Pilgrimage* (San Francisco: Harper & Row, 1989), p. 166.

7. Maryknoll, N.Y.: Orbis Books, 1991.

8. Maryknoll, N.Y.: Orbis Books, 1987.

9. See James Dunn's comments about this in *The Partings of the Ways*, especially pp. 96–97.